A Roman Miscellany

This book is respectfully dedicated
to past students of the Venerable English College
who courageously followed its motto:
Pro Petri, Fide et Patria.

A Roman Miscellany
The English in Rome, 1550–2000

edited by
Nicholas Schofield

GRACEWING

First published in 2002

Gracewing
2 Southern Avenue, Leominster
Herefordshire HR6 0QF

All rights reserved. No part of this publication may be reproduced, stored in a retrieval system, or transmitted in any form, or by any means, electronic, mechanical, photocopying, recording or otherwise, without the written permission of the publisher.

Compilation and editorial material
© Nicholas Schofield 2002

Copyright for individual essays resides with the authors. The right of the editor and the contributors to be identified as the authors of this work has been asserted in accordance with the Copyright, Designs and Patents Act 1988.

ISBN 0 85244 575 X

Typeset by Action Publishing Technology Ltd,
Gloucester GL1 5SR

Printed in England by
Antony Rowe Ltd, Eastbourne BN23 6QT

Contents

List of Illustrations	vii
Notes on Contributors	ix
Foreword	
Cardinal Cormac Murphy-O'Connor	xiii
Editor's Introduction	
Nicholas Schofield	1
Cardinal William Allen	
Eamon Duffy	11
The English College and the Martyrs' Cause	
Bishop Brian Foley	55
Cardinal Philip Howard – Rome and English Recusancy	
Judith Champ	71
'Not Accepted by Men but Chosen by the Will of God' – The Cardinal Duke of York	
Nicholas Schofield	89
Julian Watts-Russell and the Papal Zouaves	
Richard Whinder	109
John Henry Newman and the English College	
Jerome Bertram, Cong. Orat.	123
'Glorious Hopes and Designs' – the Pugins in Rome	
Carol Richardson	133
Memories of a Victorian Cardinal: Edward Howard	
Abbot Sir David Oswald Hunter-Blair, O.S.B.	157
'Dear Old Monte Porzio' – Seminarians on Vacation, 1820–1920	
Nicholas Schofield	163

'That English Romayne Life': Exile at Stonyhurst
(1940–46)
  Mgr Richard L. Stewart   179
Basil Hume Remembered
  Gerard Skinner   185
Afterword: Allen's College in Rome
  Cardinal Basil Hume, O.S.B.   197
Select Bibliography   201

Illustrations

The English College church, from a woodcut, c. 1580. Courtesy of the Venerable English College.	xii
Pope Gregory XIII and the first students of the English College. Courtesy of the Venerable English College.	10
One of the frescoes in the English College Tribune, originally painted by Pomerancio. Courtesy of the Venerable English College.	54
Cardinal Philip Howard. Courtesy of Oscott College Archives.	70
Henry Benedict Stuart, Cardinal Duke of York. Courtesy of Oscott College Archives.	88
Julian Watts-Russell in his Zouave uniform. Courtesy of the Venerable English College.	108
John Henry Newman and Ambrose St John in Rome, 1847. Courtesy of the Fathers of the Birmingham Oratory.	122
Edward Welby Pugin's 1864 neo-Gothic design for the English College church. Photograph – author's collection.	132
Cardinal Edward Howard. Courtesy of Oscott College Archives.	156
A student of the English College in 1710. Courtesy of the Venerable English College.	162

The College year of 1945–6, shortly before their
return to Rome. Photograph – editor's collection. 178

Students at St Peter's in October 1946. Photograph –
editor's collection. 183

Cardinal George Basil Hume, O.S.B. Photograph by
kind permission of the Administrator of
Westminster Cathedral. 184

Cardinal William Allen. Courtesy of the Venerable
English College. 196

Notes on contributors

Revd Jerome Bertram, Cong. Orat. is a member of the Oxford Oratory. While a student at the English College, Rome, he catalogued the archive and wrote an appendix to Michael Williams' history of the College. Since then he has published widely – on subjects as diverse as brass-rubbing, prayer and Cardinal Newman – and is a member of the Society of Antiquaries.

Dr Judith Champ is Assistant Pastoral Director and Lecturer in Church History at St Mary's College, Oscott. She formerly taught at King's College, London and recently published *The English Pilgrimage to Rome* (2000).

Dr Eamon Duffy was born in Dundalk, Ireland, and was educated at Hull and Cambridge. He has taught at Durham (1971–74), King's College, London (1974–79) and Magdalene College, Cambridge (1979–) where he is currently President. He has published widely: *The Stripping of the Altars* won the '1994 Longman's History Today Prize' for the best historical work published in Great Britain, while *Saints and Sinners* (1997) has been translated into numerous languages. He most recently published *The Voices of Morebath* (2001).

Bishop Brian Foley was born in Ilford in 1910 and lived on the same street as the future Cardinal Heenan. He was educated at Ushaw and the English College, Rome, before being ordained in 1937. In 1962 he was appointed Bishop of Lancaster and he attended all four sessions of the Second Vatican Council. He combined his pastoral duties with a great love of Catholic history – he wrote several books and founded the Essex Recusant Society. He was also President of the Catholic Record Society (1964–79) and the Catholic Archive Society (1980–99). Retiring in 1985, he kept himself active through pastoral visiting and study – indeed, shortly before his death in 1999 he managed to publish *The Story of the Jubilee Years 1300–1975*.

Cardinal George Basil Hume, O.S.B. was born in Newcastle-upon-Tyne in 1923 and was educated at Ampleforth, where he became a Benedictine novice at the age of 18. He read History at St Benet's Hall, Oxford, and studied for a licentiate in Theology at Fribourg University in Switzerland. Ordained in 1950, he was elected Abbot in 1963 and installed as ninth Archbishop of Westminster on 25 March 1976. Two months later he was created Cardinal Priest of San Silvestro in Capite by Paul VI. He was President of the Bishops' Conference of England and Wales (1979–99) and of the European Bishops' Conferences (1978–87) and won great acclaim as a spiritual leader and writer. He was awarded the Order of Merit by Her Majesty the Queen in May 1999, just weeks before his death.

Abbot Sir David Hunter-Blair, O.S.B. was born in 1853 and educated at Eton and Magdalen College, Oxford, where he is supposed to have had rooms on the same staircase as Oscar Wilde. His first trip to Rome was marked by work as a stretcher-bearer in the Siege of Rome (1870). He became a Catholic shortly afterwards and worked in the Papal service after finishing at Oxford, where he first encountered Cardinal Edward Howard. In 1878 he joined the monastery at Fort Augustus in Scotland and was ordained in 1886. Here he served as Prior (1912) and

Abbot (1913–18). He published several volumes of memoirs before his death on 12 September 1939.

Dr Carol Richardson is a Research Lecturer in Art History at the Open University. She has studied cardinals' patronage in the fifteenth century and is a frequent visitor to the English College, Rome, where she organized an Archive Conference in Spring 2002.

Revd Nicholas Schofield studied Modern History at Exeter College, Oxford, and Theology at the Pontifical Gregorian University, Rome. He co-wrote *The Forty-Four* (1999) and produced a history of the shrine of Our Lady of Willesden (2002). He also worked as Archivist at the English College, edited the 2001 issue of *The Venerabile* and is currently working in a London parish.

Mgr Richard Stewart was born in 1926 and educated at St John Fisher, Purley, before joining the English College, then in exile at Stonyhurst. He returned with the College to Rome in 1946 and was ordained at the Lateran Basilica in 1950. He later became Professor of Dogmatic Theology at Wonersh, before turning his attentions to Church Unity. He was Co-Secretary to ARCIC at the time of his unexpected death in July 1985.

Revd Gerard Skinner was Organ Scholar at Westminster Cathedral before commencing studies for the Priesthood at the English College, Rome. He took degrees in Philosophy and Theology and studied for a licentiate in Dogmatic Theology at the Pontifical Gregorian University. He is presently an assistant priest in North London.

Revd Richard Whinder studied History at King's College, London, and Theology at the Pontifical Gregorian University, Rome, where he specialized in Dogma for his licentiate. He has worked in the English College Archive, co-wrote *The Forty-Four* (1999), and is currently working as an assistant priest in Canterbury.

The English College Church from a woodcut, *c.* 1580

Foreword

In October 2001 I had the privilege of taking formal possession of my 'titular' church as a Cardinal Priest of the Holy Roman Church – Santa Maria sopra Minerva. This is a very beautiful church, as many of you will know, and at first glance may seem to be a very 'Roman' sanctuary. It boasts the body of the patron saint of Italy (St Catherine of Siena), the tomb of one of its most inspired artists (Fra Angelico) and the chapels of many local families. But, if you know where to look, there are English parts as well – most notably, the tomb of Cardinal Philip Howard, a relative of the Dukes of Norfolk who acted as Cardinal Protector of England in the late seventeenth century.

This book, *A Roman Miscellany*, is made up of historical articles that were originally printed in *The Venerabile*, the journal of the Venerable English College, Rome. They bear witness to the bonds that link our country to Rome – a city that has always belonged to everyone and a symbol of the unity that we find in Christ Jesus.

Many of the essays revolve around the English College, where I spent many happy years as a student and later as Rector. But the College has always had significance above and beyond that of a seminary, important though that might be. Claiming to be the oldest English institution overseas still in existence, it is the very embodiment of the English relationship with Rome and its history presents a fascinating sidelight on our nation's story.

I take great delight, then, in commending *A Roman Miscellany* to a wide readership. I hope that all who pick up this book will be brought to a greater appreciation of the unique role played by the Eternal City in our history and our Faith.

Cardinal Cormac Murphy-O'Connor
Archbishop's House
Westminster

Editor's Introduction

The origins of Christianity on these isles are shrouded in the mists of history. All we can safely say, Glastonbury legends aside, is that if St Alban really was martyred at the beginning of the third century, as scholars are now suggesting, then Christianity had already become a tangible presence in Britannia little over a hundred years after the death of the last of the Twelve – St John (*c*. 100).

The origins of the English in Rome are equally vague. According to a popular tradition, one of the earliest Christian households in the Eternal City was organized under the auspices of a British woman named Claudia. She was the wife of Pudens, a senator and a friend of Martial's, who memorialized Claudia in one of his epigrams:

> Though Claudia doth descend of British race,
> Yet her behaviour's full of grace;
> Her beauty far the Italian dames surpass,
> And for her wit she may for Grecian pass.

Tradition has long identified this Roman couple with the Pudens and Claudia mentioned as members of St Paul's Roman brethren in his second letter to Timothy (2 Timothy 4: 21) and the parents of Praxedes and Pudentiana, both of whom have ancient Roman churches named after them. At Santa Pudentiana – later to become the 'titular' church of Cardinal Wiseman – the visitor can still see a wooden table on which St Peter supposedly celebrated Mass. It is a curious historical possibility: that the apostolic ministries of the Galilean fisherman and the tent-maker from Tarsus were supported by this quasi-British household in the Imperial centre of Rome and that two of the city's most ancient basilicas are named after half-British maidens.

It is, however, strangely appropriate. Rome has always been an inclusive city, the *caput mundi*, with representatives of every nation calling it their home. Over the last two thousand years, the English have had a presence in Rome as pilgrims, officials, cardinals, landowners, scholars, artists, exiles, seminarians, soldiers and tourists. There has even been a pope (Adrian IV) and a pretender-king ('Henry IX'). The history of the English in Rome, then, exists on many different levels and it is hoped that this collection of essays, despite its 'miscellaneous' nature, will help readers explore some of these diverse connections and themes.

The pieces in this book were originally published in *The Venerabile*, the journal of the Venerable English College in Rome, which, since its creation in 1922 (with the exception of a brief 'blip' in the mid-1970s), has contained many articles chronicling the history of the College and of the English in Rome. The English College itself is, of course, the most concrete expression of this relationship between the English and the Eternal City. It began as the Hospice of St Thomas in 1362, offering lodgings and support for English pilgrims. Another charitable hospice, dedicated to St Edmund, was established across the Tiber in Trastevere in 1396. The two hospices merged in 1464. They could claim ancestry in the *Schola Saxonum*, a much earlier English 'colony' that had sprung up in the vicinity of St Peter's during the eighth century.

The English pilgrimage to Rome was a popular act of devotion and penance, mixed with the odd bit of shopping and sightseeing, despite the many dangers involved.

These ranged from Alpine snowstorms (which killed Archbishop Aelfsige of Canterbury in 959), and outbreaks of the plague (which claimed the life of another unlucky Archbishop, Wighard, in 668) to attacks of Saracens and of unscrupulous innkeepers. Nevertheless, the *pellegrinatio* to Rome enjoyed a distinguished pedigree. Rome proved a magnet for Saxon royalty and several kings, such as Caedwalla and Ine, made their way across the Alps and ended up being buried at St Peter's. The Tuscan town of Lucca still venerates St Richard, another royal English pilgrim who died *en route* to Rome and Jerusalem – legend refers to him as 'King of Wessex', though in reality he was probably a member of a princely family. He fathered three illustrious saints (SS Walburga, Willibald and Winnebald) and his shrine stands in the church of San Frediano – himself an Irish missionary bishop active in the area during the sixth century. The so-called 'Dark Ages' were remarkably cosmopolitan.

Royal visits to Rome ceased with the Norman Conquest, though by the fifteenth century the Hospice of St Thomas was called the 'King's Hospice', its warden being appointed by the sovereign. The medieval hospice church boasted an intriguing painting showing Richard II and Anne of Bohemia kneeling before Our Lady and, with St John the Baptist acting as mediator, offering her the royal isle with the words *'Dos tua virgo pia haec est, quare rege, Maria'* ('This is your dowry, O pious Virgin'). The painting has not been seen since the French occupation of the 1790s, but it throws considerable light on the more famous treasure of the National Gallery – 'The Wilton Diptych', painted for the king around 1395 and showing a similar scene. Referring to England as *Dos Mariae*, the Dowry of Mary, the presence of this important painting at the Hospice indicates the intimate link between England and Our Lady for our pre-Reformation forebears as well as between the Hospice and the Crown.

The sixteenth century saw a revolution for the English community in Rome. The Hospice was severely damaged by the Sack of Rome (1527) and the numbers of pilgrims, already low due to Habsburg–Valois hostilities, were brought to a virtual standstill by Henry VIII's break with Rome. The Hospice became little more than a refuge for squabbling exiles. However, its transformation into a Tridentine-style seminary in 1579 pointed to a new future. The mastermind behind this project was William Allen, who effectively saved English Catholicism from death by an injection of freshly trained seminarists. His seminaries at Douai and Rome were surrogate Oxbridges that formed the focus of a widespread English Catholic Diaspora. As Eamon Duffy explains in a fascinating article written for the four hundredth anniversary of his death, Allen was a complex character. The saviour of the English church, but also a plotter against the late Tudor regime – most clearly seen in the so-called 'Enterprise of England', which intended to place Allen back in his homeland as Cardinal Legate and Archbishop of Canterbury.

Ever since the time of Allen, the College has maintained its tradition of the 'Forty-Four' – the number of students who, led by St Ralph Sherwin, were martyred for the Faith between 1581 and 1679. Sometimes we forget the impact these executions made not only on the English Catholic community but also on the rest of Europe. Continental readers avidly devoured reports of the persecution. Allen's account of Campion's death (*A Briefe Historie*, 1582) was quickly translated into French and Spanish. No less a figure than St Francis de Sales admitted, around 1609: 'I would give my life a thousand times over to bring England back to the fold, but of course our Holy Father, the Pope, would have to be pleased to send me on the mission'. Gregory XIII gave permission for the relics of these martyrs to be placed in altars and for the martyrdoms to be depicted in churches.

The late Bishop Brian Foley, a great supporter of Catholic historical research and a distinguished old Roman, examines the emphasis placed by the Jesuits on the visual arts in their evangelization programme. The frescoes of English martyrdoms, painted for the College by Pomerancio, are an excellent example of this and later became important evidence for the beatification and canonization of the English Martyrs. Books of engravings depicting the persecution in England, such as Cavalleri's *Ecclesiae Anglicanae Trophea* (1584), based on the College frescoes, became a popular genre. One such book inspired Dom Pedro Coutinho, a retired Portuguese soldier, to fund the opening of the English College, Lisbon.

The College in Rome may have been the 'Pontifical Seminary of Martyrs', as Blessed John Cornelius dubbed it, but it was also part of the Baroque city. Andrea Pozzo not only painted the stunning fresco of the Assumption in the so-called 'Martyrs' Chapel' but planned to build an oval church, with a double dome and six chapels. The College's musical establishment used much local talent – which in the sixteenth century included the likes of Palestrina, Vittoria and Anerio, as well as home-grown musicians such as Peter Philips. Its liturgy was, likewise, fully in line with contemporary custom. In February 1626, for example, the College mourned the death of its Cardinal Protector, Oduardo Farnese. A huge catafalque was erected in the College church, complete with Farnese heraldry and skulls and cross-bones. Round about were hung sonnets composed by the students in a veritable babel of languages: Greek, Latin, Tuscan, Roman, French, English, Irish, even Welsh.

So used are we to thinking of the martyrs in terms of hiding-holes and Tyburn, that it seems almost disrespectful to imagine them celebrating the Feast of St Thomas with a High Mass *coram Cardinali* (perhaps with hired *castrati*) or wandering around the *Castelli* town of Monte Porzio during their summer *villeggiatura*.

The College also continued its medieval tradition of hospitality. The seventeenth century saw visits from curious travellers such as William Harvey (1636), John Milton (1638) and John Evelyn (1644), who recorded in his *Diary* that 'we din'd in their common Refectory, and afterward saw an Italian Comedy acted by their alumni before the Cardinals'. These dramatic productions, which were a key part of early modern Jesuit pedagogy, could be highly elaborate. The 1634 production of Joseph Simon's *Zeno*, for instance, included two dumb shows and required the use of a chariot and three harpsichords.

Despite lacking a Hierarchy, English Catholics managed to be included in the College of Cardinals during 'penal times'. In the late seventeenth century, for example, the Dominican, Philip Howard, represented English interests in Rome. Judith Champ provides a compelling account of his life and achievements, which included support for the rebuilding of the English College in the 1680s. The eighteenth century saw the long cardinalate of the Cardinal Duke of York, stretching over sixty years, even if the closest he got to stepping on British territory was his evacuation to Sicily (probably) on a British warship in 1798. The cause that he headed during the closing years of the eighteenth century added many exiles to the already well-established English Catholic Diaspora both in Rome and across Europe. The English College, like many of its sister institutions in France and Flanders, provided an important rallying point. Exposition was held at the College in 1708 for the success of the latest Jacobite enterprise and again in 1712 for the recovery of 'James III' from smallpox. Supporters of 'the good old cause' were buried in the College church, such as Thomas Dereham and Martha Swinburne. The presence of the Jacobites in Rome was witness to the fact that the English community was not just a collection of argumentative exiles but players in the complex game of eighteenth-century diplomacy and statecraft for the reverberations of the court at the Palazzo Muti could be heard in Versailles and Whitehall.

From the 1790s, we find a sudden reversal of the situation. Whereas previously the European *'ancien regime'* sheltered the English Catholic exiles from persecution, the forces of revolution made Europe a sometimes-dangerous place for this Diaspora. The English College v suppressed during the French occupation and 1818 to find a rather different Rome. While English Catholics were freed from many of their former sorrows and enjoyed a triumphalistic revival, the popes spent much of the nineteenth century fighting for their rights. If they lost their temporal power, they gained much from their new status as victims of liberalism and 'prisoners of the Vatican'. It was not only pilgrims who flocked to see these papal superstars – Richard Whinder writes about Julian Watts-Russell, a young man from Ushaw who, like hundreds of other zealous Catholics, joined a corps called the Zouaves to defend the Papacy.

Carol Richardson writes of another battle being waged in both England and Rome – that fought by the Pugins in the name of Gothic architecture. It is difficult to imagine how Edward Welby Pugin's grandiose church would have fitted into the typically Roman lineaments of the via di Monserrato, yet to the architect himself it seemed as if more than mere taste was at stake. Another great figure of the nineteenth-century 'Catholic Revival' also had numerous connections with Rome, even if we prefer to think of him as a creature of Oxford senior common rooms or of the Oratory at Birmingham. Jerome Bertram speaks eloquently of John Henry Newman's years in Rome, seen through the perspective of the College.

As we enter modern times we can utilize one of the most important aspects of *The Venerabile* over the last eighty years – as a primary source for the story of the English in Rome. The essay on Monte Porzio, for example, draws on student memories of this *casa di villeggiatura*, recorded in editions of the journal in the 1920s and 1930s as well as in student diaries from the archive. Likewise, Abbot Hunter-Blair's witty account of his youthful encounters with Edward Howard brings to life one of the least known of England's cardinals.

Finally, the late Mgr Richard Stewart briefly looks back to the days of wartime exile first at Ambleside and then at

Stonyhurst. To prepare students for their eventual return, various Roman customs were continued in the cooler climes – whether it be singing the Marian antiphon on the stairs, calling the lecture rooms *'Aula I'* and *'Aula II'* or organizing a rather unconvincing *'gita'* to Ribchester. *The Venerabile* also continued undaunted – for a publication prepared in Lancashire it showed an impressive penchant for all things Italian. Meanwhile, the College property was being transformed beyond recognition. In Rome, the buildings were turned into the *'Ospedale Principe di Piemonte'* under the care of the Knights of Malta, while Palazzola (the magnificent villa bought by Mgr Hinsley in 1920 to replace Monte Porzio) was occupied by German and then American troops. When the Rector, Mgr Macmillan, visited the villa in February 1946 he was shocked to discover a windowless chapel, a deserted Italian tank and scores of Germans buried in the apple orchard. The students returned in the autumn of that year. With their well-formed *Romanità* there were few surprises, although, as one seminarian put it, many were 'appalled to find that fact was indeed stranger than fiction' as far as the Gregorian University was concerned!

And so into the present. Cardinal Basil Hume, remembered here by Gerard Skinner, one of his students, showed just how much things had changed by the turn of the Third Millennium. Here was a Catholic Archbishop, looked up to by many as the nation's spiritual leader and so respected by the Establishment that his last official duty, a fortnight before his death, was to collect the Order of Merit from the Queen. Allen, who had spent much of his energy plotting against another Queen Elizabeth, would have been amazed. It is appropriate that the last word goes to the late Cardinal, by way of a moving sermon he preached at the College in 1994.

This *Miscellany* does not claim to be a systematic work on the English in Rome. This has been done in other volumes, most recently in Judith Champ's *The English Pilgrimage to Rome* (Gracewing, 2000). Rather, it aims to give various perspectives on the role of Rome in our nation's history, as well as giving a 'taster' of *The Venerabile* – itself, a valuable record of this venerable relationship. Many more articles could have been included, though the limits of space and the need for some consistency in both style and theme narrowed down requirements for selection. I am most grateful to all the contributors for agreeing to have their pieces included and to all those involved in the production of *The Venerabile* over the years. I would like to thank Cardinal Cormac Murphy-O'Connor for graciously providing the *Foreword* and the staff of the English College, especially the Rector, Mgr Patrick Kilgarriff, and the Bursar, Joe Coughlan, for supporting this project.

Finally, little would have been possible without the backup and wisdom of Gracewing, especially Tom Longford and Jo Ashworth.

To all old Romans and lovers of Rome, *tanti auguri* and *ad multos annos*!

Revd Nicholas Schofield

A. Gregorius XIII. Pont. Max. huius Anglorum Collegij fundator ac ......
optimus Alumnos suos Christo commendat: ut quos in Angliam ad fi...
defensionem mittit aduersus hostium insidias, atq; tormenta diuina virtute
confirmet: qua freti iam aliquot pro Catholica Romana ecclesia
fortiter occubuerunt.

B. Philippus Boncompagnus S.R.E. presb. Card. tit. S. Sixti eiusdem
Pont. Fr. Fil. Collegij Protector, et Benefactor munificentiss. idē à Deo precetur.

Pope Gregory XIII and the first students of the English College, from an engraving in Cavalleri's *Ecclesiae Anglicanae Trophea*, 1584.

Cardinal William Allen

Eamon Duffy

In May 1582 the papal Nuncio in Paris wrote to Cardinal Galli, Pope Gregory XIII's Secretary of State, to update him on yet another scheme to reconvert England and Scotland to the Catholic faith. The plan had been concocted by the Spanish Ambassador in London, Don Bernardina Mendoza, in consultation with Esme Stuart, Duke of Lennox, the French Duke de Guise, and the Jesuits William Creighton and Robert Parsons. It involved landing an invasion force of 8,000 Spanish and Italian soldiers in Scotland. Expanded to 20,000 by an expected rush of devout local recruits, this army would march south into England, overthrow Elizabeth, liberate Mary Queen of Scots, and set her on the throne. This half-baked scheme, which was welcomed by the Pope as a glorious new crusade, needed a religious figurehead who could command the loyalty of all English Catholics and serve as a rallying-point for soldiers, gentry and the devout Catholic faithful. Everyone agreed that there was only one possible choice. The President of the English College at Rheims, William Allen, should be appointed to the key post in the north of England, the bishopric of Durham. Allen, the nuncio claimed, was a man

> whose authority and reputation stand so high with the whole nation that his mere presence ... will have a

greater effect with the English than several thousand soldiers ... all the banished gentlemen bear him such reverence that at a word of his they would do anything.[1]

Five years earlier Mary Queen of Scots herself had written to Doctor Allen, expressing her conviction that 'the good opinion every one of them hath of yow' was the best hope of bringing 'reunion and reconcilement' of the faction-ridden English Catholics, and she expressed her confidence in him by giving him carte blanche to use her name in his activities.[2] In August 1587 Sixtus V recognized Allen's role in the preservation of English Catholicism by appointing him 'Cardinal of England', and he took formal direction of Roman affairs relating to England from then till his death in October 1594.

The man courted and honoured in this way by princes, popes, politicians and plotters, was a schoolmaster and pamphleteer who in another age might well have enjoyed an uneventful career in a minor academic post, or ended his days in a cathedral prebend or a north-country rectory. Instead he found himself manoeuvred by circumstance and his own strong convictions to the centre of the European stage. In the pantheon of English Catholic heroes he features as a saintly and eirenic patriarch, the founder of Douai College, and later, of the *Venerabile*, the originator of the whole notion of the Elizabethan mission, and hence the man who, more than anyone else, was responsible for turning the English Catholic community from ignoble and demoralized external conformity in their parish churches, to principled religious resistance. He wrote some of the best prose of the Elizabethan age, defending the integrity of his persecuted community, and he was one of the moving spirits behind the Rheims–Douai version of the Bible. He was a man of peace, whom Catholics of all parties and persuasions respected and obeyed, and who, so long as he lived, was able to hold together even the rival bodies of Jesuits and secular clergy. Above all, from 1574 Allen sent a stream of young priests from his Colleges to

England, in many cases to prison, torture and execution. The Elizabethan regime insisted that these men died for treason: Allen eloquently maintained that they died purely for their religion. Two generations of saints, martyrs and confessors looked to him as their spiritual inspiration, their protector, their father.

This picture of Allen is perfectly accurate as far as it goes, but it leaves a great deal out, for Allen was also a political figure of some ambivalence. From 1572 at the latest he was actively involved in a series of plots for the deposition of Queen Elizabeth and the forcible reconversion of England. In 1581 and in 1584 he published two skilled and moving defences of the non-political nature of the Catholic mission. 'No man can charge us,' he insisted, 'of any attempt against the realm or the prince's person', and he absolutely repudiated any 'mislike' of Elizabeth and her ministers 'whose persons, wisdoms, moderation and prudence in Government, and manifold graces, we do honour with al our hart in al things: excepting matters incident to Religion'.[3] But for Allen that phrase 'matters incident to Religion' was a very wide rubric, and he was being economical with the truth, to put it mildly, in affirming his loyalty and respect to Elizabeth and her ministers. For, by any standard recognized in Elizabethan England, Allen was a traitor. Even as he wrote his protestations of innocence he was up to his neck in political schemes for the deposition of Elizabeth. Sixtus V created him Cardinal of England, bad-temperedly and with some reluctance, under immense pressure from Philip II of Spain and his ambassador in Rome, Count Olivares, and Allen's appointment was universally and correctly understood as an integral part of the 'Enterprise of England', an unmistakable signal of the imminence of the Armada. Inevitably, he was intended to be Cardinal Legate and Archbishop of Canterbury when Spanish forces invaded England and reimposed Catholicism. It was Allen who was chosen to summon Englishmen to rally to the Spanish flag in 1588 in a pamphlet attack on Elizabeth so savage and so scurrilous that generations of Catholic historians preferred to believe that someone else, probably a Jesuit, had written it. For all his transparent private integrity and the undoubted warmth and generosity of his temperament, Allen is a complex figure, whose career illustrates the dilemmas, and the deviousness, forced upon good men in an age of religious violence.

I. Formation

Allen was born in 1532 into a gentry family at Rossall in the Fylde of Lancashire, one of the most conservative parts of England. Even at the end of the sixteenth century large tracts of Lancashire would be barely touched by the forces of reformation. Allen never set foot in England after his second departure for the Netherlands in 1565, and Lancashire as he remembered it in the early 1560s became his vision of grass-roots England. This England of the mind was populated by robust northern gentry and farmers who did not believe a word of the new religion whose services they were forced to attend, in contrast to the effete south with its merchants, shopkeepers and courtiers who, he knew, were much infected with heresy.[4] As late as 1584 he still cherished the illusion that the majority of the population were Catholic at heart, and that Protestantism was sustained only by 'the partiality of a few powerable persons'.[5]

Oxford had an even more profound effect on him. His early adult years were spent first as an arts student during the stormy years of the Edwardian reformation, and then as a fellow of Oriel and Principal of St Mary's Hall,[6] in the triumphant period of Catholic restoration under Queen Mary. Lancashire and Oxford marked him for life. All his essential convictions were in place by the time he was thirty, and he never abandoned or altered the perspective on English affairs and the nature of the English Reformation which he gained from his conservative home background and from the easy and almost total reversal of Protestantism in which he participated in the Marian university.

Allen went up to Oxford in 1547, took his BA in 1550, and was immediately elected fellow of his College, Oriel. To a greater extent even than Cambridge, Oxford had proved highly resistant to Protestantism, and Allen's student opinions were formed in an intensely and militantly orthodox environment. The Edwardian regime tried to bulldoze the University into the new religion by a combination of sackings and promotions. From 1548 religious controversy in Oxford was fuelled by the presence there of the Italian reformer Peter Martyr as Regius Professor of Theology. Allen's tutor, Dr Morgan Phillips, (nicknamed 'the sophister' for his debating skills) played a prominent role on the Catholic side in a great set-piece debate against Martyr at the end of May 1549.[7]

Despite Martyr's efforts and mounting government pressure, however, Oxford remained a largely Catholic university, and the accession of Queen Mary in 1553 triggered a heady period of Catholic restoration, into which Allen was quickly drawn. Two new Catholic colleges, Trinity and St John's, were founded, the latter with special provision for the teaching of canon law. Catholic scholars ousted under the Edwardian regime were restored, like Richard Smyth, who took up once again the Regius Chair from which he had been ejected in favour of Peter Martyr – Smyth would preach at the burning of Latimer and Ridley in Oxford in 1555. But the Oxford Counter-Reformation was also fed from Europe: in particular the Queen's marriage brought to the University a series of distinguished Spanish theologians. Cardinal Pole, as Chancellor of the University, appointed the Dominican Fray Bartolome Caranza, future Archbishop of Toledo and Primate of Spain, to conduct a formal visitation on his behalf to purge the University of heresy and disorder. Caranza's theological pedigree should warn us against easy assumptions that this Spanish influence was in any straightforward sense 'reactionary', for he was an Erasmian, and by the standards of the time a theological liberal. Despite his ultimately exalted office he was spectacularly to fall victim to the Spanish Inquisition in his own country, and spent the last twenty years of his life in jail. A brilliant Valladolid theologian, Juan de Villa Garcia, succeeded Smyth as Regius Professor in 1556, and was instrumental in the re-establishment of a Dominican house in Oxford in the following year. Another Dominican, Peter de Soto, reintroduced the formal teaching of scholastic theology: he was credited with restoring Oxford theology single-handedly to its pre-Reformation state of shining orthodoxy. Allen would never share the suspicion many even of his Catholic fellow-countrymen felt towards Spain and all things Spanish: he never budged from the perception of the Spaniards as champions of Catholic truth which he formed in these Oxford years.[8]

In 1556 he succeeded his tutor Morgan Phillips as Principal of St Mary's Hall, a post which involved some basic undergraduate teaching for the Arts course but was essentially that of a tutor to a couple of dozen unruly undergraduates. There, and as Proctor for two successive years, he was actively involved in the Marian purge of the University, and the religious revival which was to produce a remarkable generation of Catholic students. Among them were Gregory Martin, subsequently Allen's colleague and friend and translator of the Rheims–Douai Bible, and Thomas Stapleton, one of the most voluminous, learned and bitter-tongued of Counter-Reformation theologians. Seven products of Marian Oxford would go on to become Jesuits, nearly thirty would become seminary priests.[9]

These men of Marian Oxford were a new breed, less tolerant or at any rate less easy-going than their predecessors. Edward's reign had thrown a starker light on the choices between Rome and reformation, and issues which had been fudged or genuinely obscure in Henry's reign were now visible for what they were. Men now understood better the need to take sides, and take sides they did. Thomas Harding, who had himself been an ardent disciple of Peter Martyr and a proselytizing Protestant in Edward's reign, had not a good word for his former fellow-Protestants – they were 'theeves', 'Ministers of Antichrist', 'loose Apostates', 'apes', driven by profane malice, rancour and spite. Thomas Stapleton would one day publish an entire lecture devoted to a discussion of whether heretics were chiefly motivated by wickedness or low cunning.[10] Allen fully shared these attitudes. He was almost certainly a witness of Cranmer's Oxford trial and burning, but if so he felt no pity for the old man's agonized indecision and successive recantations, describing him later as that 'notorious perjured and oft relapsed apostate, recanting, swearing, and forswearing at every turn'.[11] He wholeheartedly endorsed the Marian Counter-Reformation, including the persecution of Protestants. Why, he asked 'should any man complain or think strange for executing the laws which are as ancient, as general and as godly against heretics as they are for the punishment of traitors, murderers, or thieves?' Those who shed their blood for heresy 'can be no martyrs but damnable murderers of themselves'.[12] For the men of his generation, there could be no halting between opinions. Right was right, wrong was wrong, and the Catholics had a monopoly on right: as Allen memorably put it, 'To be shorte, Truth is the Churchis dearlinge, heresy must have her maintenaunce abrode'.[13]

Catholicism at Allen's Oxford, then, was upbeat, pugnacious, articulate. It was also highly successful. By the end of Mary's reign not a stone was left on a stone of the Protestant coup which had taken place in Edward's reign. John Jewel told Bullinger that in the University 'there are scarcely two individuals who think with us ... That despicable friar Soto, and another Spanish monk ... have so torn up by the roots all that Peter Martyr so prosperously planted, that they have reduced the vineyard of the Lord into a wilderness'.[14] But the extent of that triumph was to become evident only when it had in turn been overthrown. Mary's reign was too short, and the millions of words of controversy in refutation of the new religion and its advocates which gushed from Allen and his colleagues, Harding, Stapleton, Sanders and Smith, in exile in the 1560s were in a sense the late-gathered first-fruits of Marian Oxford and its Counter-Reformation.

The accession of Queen Elizabeth put an end to Allen's Oxford career. Between 1559 and 1561 all but one of the Catholic heads of Colleges were ejected, and Allen left his post as Principal of St Mary's Hall. He lingered a while in the University, which remained largely Catholic in opinion despite the government purge, but in 1561 he joined the drift of displaced Marian academics to the Catholic Low Countries.[15] During the brief Protestantizing of Oxford under Edward many Oxford men had gone to the University of Louvain to continue theological work in a Catholic environment, and Louvain once more drew the new wave of Oxford exiles. Like others, Allen seems to have led a hand-to-mouth existence there, continuing the theological studies he had begun at Oxford and supplementing his income with private tutoring. In 1562 a severe bout of illness brought him home to Lancashire to convalesce, and it was here that his view of the Elizabethan Reformation took its final form.

It is now generally accepted that the Elizabethan Church took more than a decade to make serious inroads on the Catholic convictions and instincts of the population at large. What Professor Collinson has called the 'birth-pangs of Protestant England' were protracted and painful, and most of the adult population in 1559 viewed the new religious regime with something very far short of enthusiasm.[16] Yet by and large the parish clergy conformed to the new order, serving Elizabeth as they had once served Mary, and most parishioners, whatever their reservations, followed the clergy's lead and continued to attend services in their parish church. Social conformity, as much as the new twelve-penny fine for absence, brought the people to sit under the new teaching.[17]

Allen was horrified to discover these compromises among his Lancashire neighbours, where he found that not only did the majority of the Catholic laypeople attend Prayer Book services, many even communicating, but also that many priests 'said mass secretly and celebrated the heretical offices and supper in public, thus becoming partakers often on the same day (O horrible impiety) of the chalice of the Lord and the chalice of devils'. He launched a vigorous campaign to persuade them to 'abstain altogether from the communion, churches, sermons, books and all spiritual communication with heretics'. We perhaps catch an echo of the overconfidence of this cocksure young man from Oxford in his later account of how he went from one gentry household to another and 'proved by popular but invincible arguments that the truth was to be found nowhere else save with us Catholics'.[18]

Allen remained in England for three years, though his polemical activities made Lancashire too hot to hold him. He spent some time in the Oxford area, where he was able to note at first hand the persistence of Catholicism within the University, and then in the household of the officially Protestant but fellow-travelling Duke of Norfolk. In 1565, the year in which he was finally deprived of his Oriel fellowship for non-residence, he left England for the last time, settling this time in Malines where he was ordained to the priesthood, and found a teaching post in the Benedictine college there.[19]

II. Exile

Throughout these years Allen was also establishing himself as a writer. The polemical programme he developed in Lancashire was later distilled into a 'Scroll of Articles' which he himself never published, but which circulated in manuscript and which was adopted as the basis for controversial treatises by several other writers.[20]

Shortly after settling in Malines he published a treatise defending Catholic belief in Purgatory. This had been largely written three years before as a contribution to the controversy stirred up by John Jewel's *Apology* for the Church of England.[21] It is a vigorous book, which shows the ferocity of Allen's rejection of Protestantism – 'this wasting heresy, ... nothing else but a canker of true devotion, an enemy to spirituall exercise, a security and quiet rest in sinne' a 'gathered body of no faithe', taught by 'cursed Calvin ... that miserable forsaken man'.[22] It also demonstrates his way with words, and his eye for the telling phrase – as in his summary of the disastrous moral effects of the doctrine of justification by faith: 'Feasting hathe wonne the field of fasting: and chambering allmost bannished chastitye', or his contemptuous dismissal of Protestant apologists as obscure denizens of the night – 'owle light or moonshyne I trowe, or mirke midnight were more fit for theyre darke workes and doctrine, our way is over much trodden for theves'.[23]

But the *Defense and Declaration* is far more than a polemical put-down. It contains some of the richest English theological writing of the sixteenth century, and the tendency to disparage Allen as a 'mild, scholarly, rather dull man', 'in no sense distinguished' compared to the other Louvainists, altogether fails to take account of the quality of his writing.[24] He was indeed singled out by C. S. Lewis as the author of prose on a par with that of Richard Hooker,[25] and the *Defense and Declaration* in particular reveals his writing at its most powerful. Consider the theological and rhetorical splendour of this passage on the Church, which reveals, incidentally, something of his own passionate dedication to the vision of a truly Catholic Church:

> This socyety is called in oure crede, *communio sanctorum*, the communion of Sanctes, that is to say a blessed brotherhood under Christe the heade, by love and religion so wroght and wrapped to gether, that what any membre

off this fast body hath, the other lacketh it not: what one wanteth, the other suppliethe: when one smarthethe, all feeleth in a maner the lyke sorowe: when one ioyethe, thother reoisethe wythall. This happy socyety, is not inpared by any distance of place, by diversity off goddes giftes, by inequalyty off estates, nor by chaunge of liefe: so farre as the unity of goddes spirit reacheth, so farr this fellowship extendethe. This city is as large, as the benefite of Christes deathe takethe place. Yea within all the compasse of his kingdom, this fellowship is fownde. The soules and sanctes in heaven, the faithful people in earth, the chosen children that suffer chastisement in Purgatory, are, by the perfect bond of this unity, as one abundeth, redy to serve the other, as one lacketh, to crave of the other Christe oure heade, in whose bloude this city and socyety standeth, wil have no woorke nor way of salvation, that is not common to the whole body in generall, and perculierly proffitable, to supply the neede of every parte thereof.[26]

But Allen's mind was already turning to other more practical measures for the defence of Catholicism. The Elizabethan purge of the Universities had created a Catholic Diaspora in France and the Low Countries every bit as remarkable as that of the more celebrated Protestant Exiles of Mary's reign. More than a hundred senior members left the University of Oxford for religious reasons in the first decade of Elizabeth's reign, at least thirty-three from New College alone. They naturally gravitated to university towns like Louvain and, later, Douai. In 1563 Nicholas Sanders, Thomas Stapleton and John Martial, all former fellows of New College, were sharing digs in Louvain, and two short-lived houses of study were eventually formed there, nicknamed Oxford and Cambridge. John Fowler, a former New College man, set up a printing house in Louvain which published over thirty devotional and controversial works in English. Douai University, which received its charter in 1559 as the stream of refugees from the Elizabethan Settlement was just beginning, availed itself of the sudden flood of academic talent and became something of an English institution, its first Chancellor being Richard Smyth, and a number of its professors recruited from among the exiles.[27]

These exiles produced a remarkable body of controversial and devotional literature, but the potential for moral and educational disaster among them was enormous. Many had no visible means of support, many were young and in need of academic guidance and moral discipline. It appears that by the mid-1560s alms from the Catholic gentry and aristocracy in England, as well as subventions from Spain, were already being sent to support these poor scholars, but the whole process was hit and miss, and was causing trouble among the exiles.[28] It was to meet just such problems that the Halls and Colleges had emerged in the medieval Universities, and Allen felt intensely the lack of any institution offering 'regiment, discipline, and education most agreable to our Countrimens natures, and for prevention of al disorders that youth and companies of scholars (namely in banishment) are subject unto'.[29] Out of this concern Douai College emerged, and in its wake the rest of the English seminaries abroad.

III. Douai College and the Seminary Priests

The story of the founding of the English College at Douai, Allen's greatest achievement, is well-known, but Allen's precise intentions have not I think been perfectly understood.[30] By the 1580s Douai was being seen, and saw itself, as the first Tridentine seminary, and as a forcing-ground for missionary storm-troopers in the fight against Elizabethan Protestantism. But it is now generally conceded, I think too readily, that in 1568 Allen had no such thoughts in his head. In the Autumn of 1567 he made a pilgrimage to Rome, in company with his former tutor, Morgan Phillips, and a Belgian friend, John Vendeville, Regius Professor of Canon

Law at the new University of Douai, and future bishop of Tournay. Vendeville was an intensely pious Counter-Reformation activist, who wanted papal approval for a missionary enterprise to the Muslim world, but evidently did not have the right Roman connections and was refused an audience with Pius V. On their return journey Allen persuaded him to divert his interest, influence and financial backing to establishing a college for English students of theology in the Low Countries. To begin with the objectives were modest: to provide a single institution in which the scattered scholarly exiles might study 'more profitably than apart', to secure a continuity of clerical and theological training, so that there would be theologically competent Catholic clergy on hand for the good times ('were they neere, were they far of') when England returned to Catholic communion, and, finally, to provide an orthodox alternative to Oxford and Cambridge, thereby snatching young souls 'from the jaws of death'. But Vendeville would hardly have adopted the new College as a substitute project for his Barbary mission, unless he had felt that Douai itself would have some missionary dimension, and in 1568 he told the Spanish authorities in the Netherlands that the students were to be specially trained in religious controversy and, after a two-year preparation, sent back to England to promote the Catholic cause 'even at the peril of their lives'.[31] Much has been made of the apparent difference of vision between Vendeville and Allen, with Allen seen as an unimaginative conservative, intending nothing much more dynamic than St Mary's Hall or Oriel in exile. He himself later claimed that at this stage, while he thought they should be ready to seize any opportunity to promote the faith in England, nothing much could be done 'while the heretics were master there'. John Bossy, in a brilliant discussion of Allen's intentions, suggested that he was still trapped in the static theological vision of the Marian Church, unable to think of the Church working as anything other than an Establishment backed by the Crown, and so unable to conceive of mission as such, and that he only slowly came round to Vendeville's more activist conception. Indeed Bossy sees this as a watershed between Marian and Elizabethan Catholicism, with the newer missionary spirit represented by Elizabethans like Gregory Martin and Edmund Campion, men with more in common with their puritan opposite numbers in England than with the older Louvain exiles, and who, almost as much as their Protestant sparring partners, had 'no ties with the Marian Establishment, and [who] treated it with some contempt'.[32] This is certainly to drive too sharp a wedge between Marian and Elizabethan Catholicism. The Marian regime at Oxford was, as we have seen, anything but moribund or static. Gregory Martin himself was its product, and nearly forty others would become seminary or Jesuit priests. It is true that Allen's later description of his thinking about this time plays down his own missionary awareness, and so lends support to a conservative reading of the foundation of Douai, but that description comes in a letter where he is complementing Vendeville by attributing all the foresight to him. We should not in any case lay too much stress on the absence of the vocabulary of mission in Allen's utterances. As late as June 1575 he described the College as 'this college for English theologians, this refuge of exiles, this seat and home of Catholics, this place of true worship for those who have left the Samaria of the Schismatics and who have the faces of those going to Jerusalem'.[33] That last phrase, with its deliberate allusion to Jesus' journey to Jerusalem and his passion in Luke's Gospel, hints at confrontation, but the rhetoric as a whole doesn't suggest much missionary awareness, and it comes in a letter in which Allen talks of Douai simply as a place of Catholic education which will save souls who would otherwise have been led astray at Oxford or Cambridge. Yet by the time the letter was written he had already begun to send priests back to England, and, as we shall see, by now was most certainly thinking of the active reconversion of England by every means available, from bibles to bullets.

And in fact from a very early stage Allen and his fellow

exiles were aware of a missionary dimension to any such enterprise in theological education, though they had difficulty in formulating it explicitly. In 1568 an anonymous memorandum written in Allen's circle, if not by Allen himself, asked either that the English Hospice in Rome should become a seminary both for established scholars and young hopefuls, who might be theologically trained for the overthrow of heresy, or else that its revenues should be diverted to support the work just being begun at Douai, which would provide 'ideally qualified workers' when England should once again 'emerge' from heresy. The word 'emerge' suggests that the memorialist had no very clear view of how the 'emerging' might happen, but theology, controversy and mission – or at any rate the overthrow of heresy – were firmly if vaguely linked by this stage.[34] That link rapidly resolved itself into a recognized need for missionaries in England. By 1572 some of the English Louvainists, describing themselves as 'the College of Preachers', were asking for papal support for the formal establishment of an English College there, whose primary purpose would be to provide preachers and catechists for the scattered English exile communities in Europe, but which would also undertake to send missionaries to England.[35]

In these years of confusion and improvisation, then, it looks as if even some of the older activists among the exile community were feeling their way towards the conception of the Mission to England: we are not dealing here with a distinctively 'Elizabethan' invention into which Marian veterans, even relatively young veterans like Allen, were dragged, blinking and mumbling. And in fact we know that even before his trip to Rome with Vendeville, Allen was well aware of the damaging consequences of any merely passive 'waiting game'. In the preface to his treatise on the priesthood, written during Lent 1567, he lamented the 'great desolation of christian comfort and all spiritual functions' which the Elizabethan Settlement had brought to the parishes, and the dangers of leaving the people to the ministrations of schismatic and heretical parish clergy. He saw quite clearly that time mattered, and that the acceptance of the ministry of these clergy would ultimately attach the Catholic population to the new Church. 'For how can it be otherwise', he wrote. 'Baptisme is ministered by heretikes, they helpe forth such as passe hence, they keepe visitation of the sicke ... and to be short, they minister the mysteries of holy communion: so that, in time, though the libertie of Christes religion be restored againe, the youth shal take such likinge in heretikes practices, to whom by love and custom, they are so fast knit, that it will be hard to reduce them home to truth againe'.[36] Given such a perspective, the emergence of something approaching the Elizabethan mission seems inevitable: it is a short step from this sort of awareness to the frame of mind reflected in the saying recorded by the preacher at his funeral – 'it's no good waiting for better times, you have to make them happen'.[37]

The College began in a hired house near the Theological Schools in Douai at Michaelmas 1568, and received papal approval the same year. Allen was joined by a handful of former Oxford academics and a couple of Belgian theology students, for Vendeville envisaged a role for the house in training storm troopers for the northern European Counter-Reformation in general, though the Belgians soon tired of the austere conditions in the house and took themselves off. Despite contributions from local religious houses, its funding was from the start precarious, though Allen's appointment to the Regius Chair in Theology in 1570 put the house's finances on a slightly better footing. Nevertheless, the College quickly began to attract other exiles, including celebrities like Thomas Stapleton, who took up residence as 'tabler' or paying guest in 1569.[38] In 1570 Morgan Phillips died and left his entire estate to the College: on the strength of the legacy eight new theology students were taken in, including Gregory Martin and Edmund Campion. The growing numbers and the mixed character of the community called for miracles of tact on

Allen's part: he encountered widespread incomprehension and outright hostility. Some of the former Marian dignitaries among the exiles suspected him of self-aggrandizement, or of designs on the alms and pensions for which they jostled: the grant of the pope's pension in 1575 rankled particularly. To counter such suspicions, and to tempt established scholars to join in the project, Allen treated the senior recruits with almost exaggerated deference, and kept the regime of the house flexible. 'A little government ther is and order', he wrote in 1579,

> but no bondage nor straitenes in the world: ther is nether othe, nor statute, nor other bridle nor chasticement but reason and every man's conscience in honest superiority and subalternation eche one towardes other. Confession, communion, exhortation hath kept us this ix yeare I thanke God in great peace amongest ourselves, in good estimation abrode, with sufficient lyvelihod from God, and in good course of service towardes the Church and our contry.[39]

Although it has now been demonstrated that the actual numbers of priests sent from Douai and the later Colleges to England has been overestimated,[40] the growth of the College between 1570 and 1580 is an astonishing story. Recruitment was very varied. Some were gentlemen's sons, in search of a Catholic education unobtainable in England, and who came often in defiance of conformist families, fearful of government attention. There was a continuing haemorrhage from the English Universities, especially Oxford, which Allen encouraged and exploited, and which brought to Douai not only Martin and Campion, but the proto-martyr of the seminaries, Cuthbert Mayne, a graduate of St John's College and, like a good many of the early recruits, a priest of the new Church. Some of these men were already convinced Catholics, some were seekers 'doubtful whether of the two religions were true'. Allen claimed that many were schismatics or heretics, disgusted with the collapse of moral and academic standards in reformation Oxbridge, some even mainly in search of educational bursaries, an attraction which became greater after 1575, when the Pope settled a monthly pension of one hundred crowns on the College. He rejoiced in the despoiling of the Protestant Universities and set himself 'to draw into this College the best wittes out of England', a pardonable boast given the calibre of men like Martin and Campion.[41] He deliberately exploited the evangelistic potential of these young men, setting them to write to friends, family and former teachers and colleagues to urge them to become Catholics, even to 'make for once a trial of our mode of life and teaching'. The most spectacular example of this technique was the letter Campion wrote from Douai to his friend and patron Bishop Cheney of Gloucester, urging the old man to follow his secret convictions, renounce heresy and 'make trial of our banishment'.[42] The College acted as a magnet for other English exiles in the Low Countries, and had a resident local English satellite community which included a number of gentry families. It also had a stream of visitors, ranging from the casually curious about an increasingly notorious institution, to relatives or friends of the students. All were welcomed and pressed to take instruction in the faith: poor visitors were given a month's free board and lodging, a course of religious instruction, and the offer of reconciliation and the sacraments. By May 1576 there were 80 students in the College, by September the same year 120. The growing numbers created constant problems of accommodation and finance, and the foundation of the *Venerabile* was among other things an attempt simply to deal with the overflow. Nevertheless Allen resisted pressure to set fixed limits on the intake, since so many of those who came were refugees who had no other resource, or waverers who might lapse back into Protestantism if turned away. At the end of the decade he reckoned that there were on average 100 students in the College in any one year, and that they were ordaining 20 men to the priesthood annually. The first four priests left the College for England in 1574, and by 1580 about 100 in all had been sent on the Mission.[43]

The regime devised by Allen for his men is very striking, and differed in several important ways both from university theology courses and from the normal seminary syllabus of the late sixteenth century.[44] Late medieval training manuals for priests emphasized practical skills – seemly performance of the liturgy and sacramentals, basic expertise in hearing confessions, and a grounding in the essential elements of catechesis. To these Allen added an overwhelming emphasis on expertise in the Bible, a good grounding in dogmatic theology through the study of St Thomas, and constant practice in preaching and in disputation. He was intensely aware of the crucial importance of the English Bible to the success of the English Reformation, and was determined to eliminate the advantage this gave Protestants. The publication of Gregory Martin's translation of the New Testament in 1582 was part of this project, but even before its appearance Allen saw to it that his men had the Bible at their fingertips. Between three and five chapters of the Old or New Testaments were read aloud at each of the two main daily meals, followed while still at table by an exposition of part of what had been read, during which students were expected to have their bibles open before them and pen and ink to hand. In three years the students heard the Old Testament read through in this way twelve times, the New Testament sixteen times. Each was expected to do private preparatory work on the passages read communally, there was a daily lecture on the New Testament, Hebrew and Greek classes, and regular disputations on the points of scripture controverted between Catholics and Protestants. There were two lectures each day on St Thomas, and a weekly disputation on points from the week's lectures. The men also studied Church history, especially English Church history, the canons and decrees of Trent, and the catechisms of Trent and of Peter Canisius, and they received practical instruction in the techniques of catechesis. There was a strong emphasis on the reconciliation of penitents in confession, and so on moral theology and cases of conscience, using the standard textbook of the day by the Navarese theologian Azpilcueta, supplemented by cases of conscience specially devised with the English mission in mind.[45]

To this new style theological training he added a new spirituality, focused on daily mass and regular weekly communion, twice-weekly fasting for the conversion of England, regular meditation on the mysteries of the Rosary. A fundamental element in this new, more intense piety was the use of confession as a means of spiritual growth 'not in a perfunctory way as we used to do when for custom's sake we confessed once a year'. That dismissal of the medieval Sarum past is significant. Allen believed that the Reformation was a judgement on the sins and superficiality of the people, and so a deeper, more self-conscious penitence was a necessary condition of the restoration of Catholicism. For this purpose he specially valued the Jesuit Spiritual Exercises 'in order to the perfect examination of our consciences' and the choice of 'a holier state of life'.[46]

In the early days of the seminary Allen's recruits were a miscellaneous lot, from seasoned and sometimes very senior academics to raw lads from country grammar schools. He was realistic about what could be achieved with much of the material he had to hand: Mercury, he told a critic of the seminary, 'cannot be made of every 1099'.[47] He was in the business of producing 'plaine poor priests', for whom 'zeal for God's house, charity and thirst for souls' were more important than academic achievement. Nevertheless, he knew quite well that his regime was producing a different kind of priest, more professional, better instructed, altogether more formidable 'than the common sort of curates had in old tyme'. He thought his men compared well with those emerging from any seminary in Europe, and even in some respects with the Jesuits, for whom he had an unqualified reverence and admiration. He believed in the special value of a graduate clergy, and academic distinction was highly prized at Douai: Masters of Arts and Doctors at Douai were appointed humbler students as servitors to wait on them at table, and sat in due order of precedence at high table. As long as funds were available for it, members of the college were encouraged to take theological degrees in the University of Douai, and Cuthbert Mayne kept the exercise for his baccalaureate in theology just days before returning to England and martyrdom in 1575. There is no doubt that this emphasis on theological excellence derived directly from Allen himself, and was part of the legacy of Marian Oxford to the Elizabethan mission. By contrast, graduates going from Douai to Rome noticed and frequently resented the lack of deference the Jesuit regime there paid to scholastic distinction.[48] Allen regretted the way in which missionary demands and funding priorities inexorably forced the theological concerns of the College to the margins, and nursed a project for a College where English priests might pursue advanced theological studies.[49] In all this he also had his eye on Elizabethan Oxford and Cambridge, and the need to excel them, above all in their boasted excellence in scripture. There were more and better theological courses, including training in scripture, he claimed, 'in our two colleges, then are in [the Protestants'] two Universities conteining neere hand 30 goodly Colleges'.[50]

By the same token he was impatiently dismissive of nostalgic comparisons made by his fellow-Catholics – 'that golden world is past, yf ever any such were'.[51]

He resented the criticism, made by conservatives like the veteran English Carthusian, Maurice Chauncey, of the youth, inexperience and unpriestly deportment of the seminarians going in 'disguised gear' of ruffs and feathers on the mission. For above all Allen was intensely aware of the dangers his men incurred. It has been calculated that of the 471 seminary priests known to have been active in England in Elizabeth's reign, at least 294 (62%) were imprisoned at some time or another. 115 fell into government hands within a year of arrival, 35 actually while still in the ports at which they landed. 116 were executed, 17 died in gaol, 91 were banished, of whom 24 subsequently returned at great risk. Allen worried about the power of life and death he exercised over these men. When in 1585 twenty of them were expelled from England and duly reported to Allen for duty, he did not feel he had the right to send them back on the mission: in his last years in Rome as a cardinal he would contrast the comfort and safety of his own life with the danger and suffering of his priests.[52] Most men, he told Chauncey,

> mark there [their] misses, and few consider in what feares and daungers they be in and what unspeakable paines they take to serve good menns tomes to there least perill. I could recken unto youe the miseryes they suffer in night journeyes, in the worst wedder that can be picked; perill of theves, of water, of watches, of false brethrene; there close abode in chambers as in pryson or dongeoon withowt fyre and candell leest they gyve token to the enemy where they bee; there often and sudden raisinge from there bedds att mydnight to avoyde the diligent searches of haeretikes; all which and divers other discontentments, disgraces and reproches they willinglye suffer, which is great penannce for there fethers, and all to wynne the soweles of there dearest countreyemen.[53]

Yet these sufferings were fundamental to the spirituality Allen encouraged among the seminarians, and to the message he wished through them to impress upon the Catholics in England. Their sufferings, he told his priests, were stronger intercession for their country 'than any prayers lightly in the world' – 'Bloude so yielded maketh the forciblest meane to procure mercie that can be'. The likelihood of martyrdom was actually one of the inducements Allen offered to persuade Campion to go to

England, and in the wake of his and his companions' executions Allen told the Rector of the *Venerabile* that 'Ten thousand sermons would not have published our apostolic faith and religion so winningly as the fragrance of these victims, most sweet both to God and men'. He was distributing fragments of Campion's 'holy ribbe' as relics by May 1582.[54] Some of his most moving writing occurs in the exhortation to constancy in martyrdom with which the Apologie for the two Colleges ends:

> Our daies can not be many, because we be men: neither can it be either godly or worldly wisdom, for a remnant of three of foure yeres, and perchance not so many monethes, to hazard the losse of all eternity. They can not be good in these evil times ... And were they never so many or good, to him that refuseth his faith and Maister, they shal never be joyful, but deadly and doleful. Corporally die once we must every on and but once, and thereupon immediatly judgement, where the Confessor shal be acknowledged, and the Denyer denyed againe.
>
> No Martyrdom of what length or torment so ever, can be more grevous, then a long sicknes and a languishing death: and he that departeth upon the pillow, hath as little ease as he that dieth upon the gallowes, blocke, or bouchers knife. And our Maisters death, both for paines and ignominie, passed both sortes, and all other kinds either of Martyrs or malefactors. Let no tribulation then, no perill, no prison, no persecution, no life, no death separate us from the charity of God, and the society of our sweete Saviours passions, by and for whose love we shal have the victory in all these conflictes.[55]

The whole seminary project was in a sense heroic, confrontational, its objective the separation of the Catholic community from an acquiescent conformity which, he understood perfectly well, would ultimately absorb and undo them: And so his men were nursed not only in readiness for martyrdom, but in a robust hatred of Protestantism.

> By frequent familiar conversations we make our students thoroughly acquainted with the chief impieties, blasphemies, absurdities, cheats and trickeries of the English heretics, as well as with their ridiculous writings, sayings and doings. The result is that they not only hold the heretics in perfect detestation, but they also marvel and feel sorrow of heart that there should be any found so wicked, simple and reckless of their salvation as to believe such teachers, or so cowardly and worldly-minded as to go along with such abandoned men in their schism or sect, instead of openly avowing to their face the faith of the catholic church and their own.[56]

That was the point – to bring the laity to see the necessity of recusancy, of making a clean break with the parish churches, thereby ensuring the survival of an uncompromised Catholicism. Less than ten years after the establishment of Douai Allen could rejoice that 'innumerable nowe confesse there faithe and abhorreth all communion and participation with the sectaryes in there servyce and sacraments, that before, beinge catholykes in there hart, for worldly feare durst not so doo'.[57] Insistence on this point was a major theme in the writings of Allen and his circle, and in the casuistic formation of the seminary priests themselves,[58] but it was uphill work, and through his own conviction, Allen understood the pressures Catholics in England were under. His last briefing with each of his priests on their departure for the mission concerned 'how and where to condiscende withowt synne to certain feablenesse growne in manns lyfe and manners these ill tymes, not always to be rigorous, never over scrupulous, so that the churche discipline be not evidently infringed, nor no acte of schisme or synne plainly committed'.[59] This should not be interpreted as willingness to legitimate church-papistry or occasional conformity, but he did his best to meet the realities of the English situation. When the draconian law imposing a £20 fine on recusants for persistent non-attendance was passed in 1581 Allen responded to lay panic by seeking some relaxation of the Vatican line on this matter, lobbying the Nuncio in Paris and consulting the leading Jesuit casuist. He was clearly relieved at the refusal of the authorities to soften their line, however, and told the Jesuit Rector of the *Venerabile* that 'no other decision was possible'.[60] Yet if connivance was forbidden, compassion was not. As persecution mounted in the early 1590s he instructed his priests to hold the line on the sinfulness of outward conformity, yet to deal gently with those who fell into it through fear – 'be not hard nor roughe nor rigorous ... in receavinge againe and absolving them ... which mercie you must use, thoughe they fall more than once, and though perhaps you have some probable feare that they will of like infirmity fall againe ... *tutior est via misericordiae quam justitiae rigoris*'.[61]

IV. The Enterprise of England

And the question of confrontation and constancy in the faith brings us at last to Allen's politics, for all his politics were tuned to the reconversion of England.

The first thing to be said is that Allen believed that he knew how to convert England: between 1553 and 1558 he had seen it done and had taken part in the process. He never doubted that what was needed for the success of this great work of God was, in essence, the repetition of the Marian restoration, and in 1588, when the Armada was about to sail, he sent for the complete Vatican files on the Legatine mission of Cardinal Pole.[62] His blueprint for the reconversion included the removal of Queen Elizabeth, and the implementation of a sternly Catholic regime. He did not believe in the toleration of error, and he did not believe that Catholics and Protestants could live in peace together. In this last, it has to be said, he had history, observation and cold common sense on his side. North-Western Europe in the 1560s and 1570s and after seemed to be falling apart at the seams for the sake of religion – France was descending into religious civil war, and his arrival in the Low Countries coincided with the outbreak of the Calvinist revolt which would separate the northern provinces from Spanish rule and the Catholic faith. From the moment of his settlement in the Low Countries, Allen's personal well being, the existence of his College and the future of his projects for the reconversion of England were inextricably involved with the political dominance of Spain. Spain's weakness was his College's peril, as he discovered when in 1578 the English College was forced by the ebb and flow of the Revolt to abandon Douai and take up temporary residence at Rheims.[63]

In the early 1560s the loyalty of Catholics was hardly an issue: the possibility of the death, the Catholic marriage or the conversion of the Queen had not yet been ruled out, and the main preoccupation of the exiles was the polemical campaign against the new religion, and the simple business of survival. But the arrival of Mary Queen of Scots in England in 1568, the Rising of the Northern Earls in 1569, and the excommunication of the Queen the following year changed all that. The Elizabethan regime was bound to treat Catholicism as a political threat, and Catholics were bound to take stock of the courses of action open to them. By now it was clear to everyone that the Elizabethan Settlement was not just going to go away. Something would have to be done, and the key to what might be done was the Bull of excommunication.

Regnans in Excelsis solemnly declared the Queen an apostate from the Catholic faith, a heretic, and a tyrant, and it absolved English Catholics of their allegiance to her. But it was issued quite irresponsibly, without any serious attempt to secure political help from Spain or anywhere else to enforce it. It therefore made the conditions of English Catholics much worse, exposing them to charges of treason without any compensating hope of liberation. It also created serious problems of conscience for them: it was clear that they need not now obey the Queen, but would they themselves incur excommunication if, out of fear, prudence, or natural loyalty they did obey her? In 1580 a ruling was secured from Gregory XIII which absolved Catholics from obedience to the Bull until its enforcement became practicable, and in the meantime it was tacitly allowed to drop. There were theologians, in any case, who questioned the extent of the Pope's authority in matters of civil allegiance, and therefore the legitimacy of the Bull.[64]

But Allen was not among them. An ardent papalist, who saw in the Pope the surest defence of the Church and the 'rocke of refuge in doubtful daies and doctrines', he was to place the excommunication and deposition of Elizabeth, and the theoretical and practical right of the Pope to perform such an act, at the centre of his political thinking.[65] In 1572 he was one of the signatories of a petition from a group of exiles at Louvain to Pope Gregory XIII, asking him to take some action to implement the Bull against the 'pretended Queen', and to extirpate Protestantism in England, from which the infection of heresy was spreading like cancer to the surrounding nations. In 1584, in a pamphlet defending the loyalty of English Catholics, he would devote three chapters to an extended defence of the deposing power of the Pope.[66] Yet it was one thing to accept *Regnans in Excelsis* and another thing to act on it, and here the only realistic hope was to involve the King of Spain. Allen was in any case in constant touch with Spain and Spanish officials in northern Europe by virtue of his growing position of leadership among the exiles: the management of pensions, the procurement of ecclesiastical and civil preferment for his growing circle of supplicants and clients, above all the protection of his College, demanded it. But he went beyond this, and throughout the 1570s and early 1580s, Allen was a key figure in a succession of plans for a Spanish invasion of

England. Early in 1576 he took part in a consultation in Rome on English affairs: the foundation of the *Venerabile* was one consequence of this visit.[67] But that was a by-product of what was in fact a council of war, whose main outcome was a plan for an invasion of England by a papal force led by Don John of Austria, to set Mary on the throne. Allen prepared a lengthy document of advice for this invasion, the first of many, in which, among other things, he suggested that the expenses should be met from the confiscated property of Protestant ecclesiastics.[68] For any such plan the support of Philip II was essential, but Spanish problems in the Netherlands meant that in the event nothing was done, and Allen was increasingly aware that simple reliance on Spain would be a mistake. However zealous for religion he might be, Philip was a politician first – as Allen's friend Nicholas Sander told him, 'wee shall have no stedy comfort but from God, in the Pope not the King of Spain. Therefore I beseech you, take hold of the Pope'.[69]

Allen's own involvement in political schemes was not continuous: his part in the invasion plans of 1576 was almost certainly directly provoked by an attempt of Elizabeth's ministers to secure an agreement with Spain for the expulsion of the exiles, in particular the College, from the Low Countries. But the wave of persecution which followed the arrival of Campion and Parsons in 1580 pushed him in this direction again. His letters in the wake of the martyrdom of Campion are a curious mixture of grief, anger and exaltation, but there is no mistaking the growth of his hostility to Elizabeth, 'our Herodias', who bathed her hands in the 'brightest and best blood' of Catholics.[70] In 1583 he was actually named as Papal Legate and Bishop of Durham in the event of the success of the proposed invasion by the Duc de Guise with which this paper began, but the discovery of the Throckmorton plot prevented its implementation.[71] 'If [the enterprise of England] be not carried out this year', he told Cardinal Galli in April 1584, 'I give up all hope in man and the rest of my life will be bitter to me'.[72] His political involvements in the fight against international Protestantism deepened, and he was drawn into the negotiations which led to the formation of the Catholic Holy League in France in 1584 and 1585.[73] In these years Allen exerted all his influence to commit the King of Spain and the Pope to the 'Enterprise of England', and his postbag was stuffed with the explosive matter of high espionage: when he fell seriously ill in the summer of 1585 he panicked and burned everything, including his cipher books.[74]

The election of a new Pope, Sixtus V, in 1585 brought the still convalescent Allen hurrying to Rome, partly to secure continued papal support for the College, but largely for political reasons. If the enterprise of England was to become a reality, the Pope had to be persuaded of its importance. Allen worked hard to scotch rumours of the easing of persecution in England, in case these should cool enthusiasm for the invasion, and in September 1585 he drafted an elaborate memorial for the Pope, describing the religious geography of England, pressing on him the widespread support in the north and west of the country for Catholicism, the unwarlike character of the urban supporters of Protestantism and the 'common and promiscuous multitude', the ease with which an invasion might be carried through.[75]

The Franciscan Pope Sixtus V was a volatile and formidable figure who was deeply committed to the recatholicizing of Europe, but he distrusted the dominance of Spain, and resented the interference of Philip in ecclesiastical affairs. If he was to be brought to back – and to help finance – the enterprise of England, every ounce of pressure and persuasion would be needed. The Spanish ambassador in Rome, Count Olivares, recognized the role Allen could play in this, and detained him in Rome. There is no doubt that he now became, to all intents and purposes, a Spanish servant, receiving detailed briefings from the cack-handed Olivares on the management of the Pope.[76] Allen's own centrality to the enterprise, in any case, was obvious, and became critical after the execution of Mary Queen of Scots: as the unquestioned religious leader of the English Catholics, he was now the only conceivable figurehead for a crusade. But if he was to serve that role he would need to be more than Dr Allen: he had to be made a cardinal. Sixtus V bowed to immense Spanish pressure, orchestrated in part by Robert Parsons, Allen's closest collaborator, and he created Allen cardinal in August 1587. Elaborate plans for his role in the invasion were drawn up, in part at least based on Pole's Legatine mission: interestingly, Allen intended to hold the office of Lord Chancellor as well as that of Archbishop of Canterbury.[77] There is no doubt in all this that the Pope saw Allen as a Spanish stooge, and when in October 1588, at Philip II's command, he sought permission to go to the Netherlands to be in readiness when the call to England came, Sixtus V threw a series of spectacular tantrums, abusing Allen, according to Olivares, 'like a Negro'.[78]

It is against these developments that we have to assess Allen's role not only in politics in general, but in the martyrdom of his priests. In the face of the Elizabethan regime's insistence that the priests died for treason, Allen eloquently maintained their total innocence. In 1581 and again in 1584 he published pamphlets claiming that none of the priests had any political involvement, and in these works and in his account of the martyrdoms of Campion and his companions he insisted that it was the government, not the Catholics, who were making an issue of the Bull of Excommunication, which Catholics had allowed to fall into a harmless oblivion. He insisted that no discussion of the Bull was allowed at Douai, and this was certainly true.[79] Yet he himself repeatedly defended the validity of the Bull in the published writings which his priests helped circulate in England, and he actively sought the armed implementation of the Bull and the deposition of Elizabeth in 1572, 1576, 1583, 1586, and 1588. In 1586, moreover, he told the Pope that the 'daily exhortations, teaching, writing and administration of the sacraments ...

of our priests' had made the Catholics in England 'much more ready' for an invasion, and that no good Catholic now 'thinks he ought to obey the queen as a matter of conscience, although he may do so through fear, which fear will be removed when they see the force from without'. The priests, he added 'will direct the consciences and actions of the Catholics ... when the time comes'. This perception of the role of the clergy was generally shared by the Catholic authorities: when the invasion by De Guise was being planned three years earlier, the Nuncio in Paris told the Cardinal Secretary of State that the leading Catholics would be informed *'per via de sacerdoti'* – through their priests.[80]

Yet Allen was not lying: he rigorously kept from all but a handful of his friends and his pupils any knowledge of his own political activities, and certainly approved of the breve of Gregory XIII formally allowing the Excommunication to be held in abeyance indefinitely, which Campion and Parsons took with them to England in 1580.[81] He himself observed a scrupulous distinction in his writings between the work of priests – which was to preach the Gospel and to endure martyrdom for it when the time came – and the role of princes and fighting-men: 'the spiritual [sword] by the hand of the priest, the [material] sword by the hand of the soldier'.[82]

The 'readiness' his priests contributed to, therefore, was indirect, a strengthening of loyalty to the papacy, and a willingness to choose God rather than man when put to the test, as the Henrician and Edwardian Catholics had so signally failed to do. The English Reformation was for him a blasphemous and sacrilegious invasion of the spiritual sphere by the secular power. It followed that any recovery of Catholic understanding and commitment, however a-political and spiritual its ministers, methods and aims, must inevitably lead to a confrontation with the Protestant state. The more clearly the people saw in the light of the Gospel, the more resolutely they would reject the claims of the royal supremacy over their consciences. A straight line runs from Allen's efforts in the early 1560s to persuade his Lancashire neighbours out of their token conformity, to his promotion of the enterprise of England in the 1580s, and the spiritual mission of the seminary priests lies squarely along that line.

But in any case the whole notion that a Catholic might be rebellious seemed to him a nonsense. It was the Protestants who were rebels, 'opinionative and restless brains to raise rebellion at their pleasure under pretense of religion', following 'their own deciptful wils and uncertaine opinions, without rule or reason', stirring up civil war in France, rebellion against the lawful sovereign in the Netherlands and in Scotland, fastening on the weakness of the body politic – 'they make their market most', he claimed, 'in the minority of princes or of their infirmity'. Catholics, by contrast, as men of 'order and obedience', took no such liberties, but 'commit the direction of matters so important to the Church and to the chief governors of their souls'. The deposing power was a God-appointed safeguard, stretching back to Old Testament priests and prophets like Samuel, and entrusted to the Pope for the preservation of the prince and people in due obedience to the law of Christ. Catholics therefore proceed by reason and conscience, Protestants by 'fury and frenzy'.[83] It was the Elizabethan government, then, with its murder of priests and war against Catholic truth which sinned, in forcing Catholic men and women to choose between civil and religious obedience, between God and the prince.

These views were never concealed by Allen – he proclaimed them in the works he published in the early 1580s: but their consequences were finally spelled out in the two open calls to resistance which he produced in 1587 and 1588. In 1587 an English commander with the Earl of Leicester's expedition to help the rebels in Holland, Sir William Stanley, surrendered the town of Deventer to the Spanish forces. Allen published a defence of his action, claiming that the English involvement in a war against Philip was sinful and unjust, Stanley's action that of an informed conscience, and that any Catholic should do the same. He further declared that 'al actes of iustice within the realme, done by the Quenes authoritie, ever since she was, by publike sentence of the Church, and Sea Apostoloke, declared an Haeretike ... and deposed from al regal dignitie ... al is voide, by the lawe of God and man ...' He called for the formation of companies of English soldiers on the Continent to be trained 'in Catholike and old godly militare discipline', just as the seminaries were training priests, to undo the evil of the Reformation: 'it is as lawful, godly and glorious for you to fight, as for us Priestes to suffer, and to die'. To labour in either of these ways for the defence of the faith 'is alwaies in the sight of God, a most precious death, and martyrdom'.[84] In the following year finally Allen burned his boats with his *Admonition to the Nobility and People of England*, calling on them to join the Spaniards and overthrow Elizabeth, whom he denounced as a sacrilegious heretic, an incestuously begotten bastard, guilty not only of oppressing the people but of ruining the commonwealth by a whole range of ills, from the promotion of base-born upstarts to the enjoyment of nameless acts of sexual debauchery with her young courtiers.[85]

There is no doubt that his political involvements contributed to the sufferings of his priests, for the Elizabethan government knew about his activities, and guessed a good deal more. Yet his priests shared with Allen a sense of the spiritual issues at stake, and the dilemmas on which they were impaled were not of his nor their making. For him and for them there could be no peace with a state which claimed an absolute authority over their consciences: his perception of that claim, and his solution to the dilemma it posed, was not so very different from that of Bonhoeffer in our own times.

Yet if in the conditions of his own time he can hardly be blamed for seeking to overthrow Elizabeth, so that the Gospel might be free, Allen cannot entirely be absolved of responsibility for the disasters of Catholicism in the 1580s and 1590s. He can be blamed, I think, for his lack of realism about the likelihood of the success of any such attempts. We are less prone now to dismiss the optimism of Elizabethan Catholics about the persistence of widespread sympathy for the old religion among the people at large: there was nothing inevitable or easy about the triumph of the Reformation. But, perhaps in part at least to counter a growing scepticism at the Spanish court about support for the enterprise, Allen persisted in the conviction that even into the mid 1580s two-thirds of the people were Catholics in their hearts and so discontented with Elizabeth's rule,[86] the 'pure zelous heretikes' 'very few' and 'effeminate, delicate and least expert in the wars'. He persuaded himself that the indifferent remainder 'will never adore the sun setting, nor follow the declining fortune of so filthie, wicked and illiberal a Creature' as Elizabeth.[87] Dazzled by the extraordinary impact of his priests, he never grasped, or allowed himself to acknowledge, the extent of anti-Spanish feeling in England, or the unlikelihood of the population of late Elizabethan England flocking to the Pope's banner. And he consistently underestimated his enemy, declaring in 1581 that no intelligent person could be a Protestant: even the promoters of reformation were certainly mere *politiques* 'who, because they be wise, can not be Protestants 23 yeres, that is to say, any long time together'.[88] It is easy with hindsight to be superior about this.

Successive popes and the most experienced king in Christendom took the same optimistic view as Allen of the prospects of success, and Philip committed the seaborne might of the world's greatest power to it. And Allen was driven by longing for restoration and return, the restoration of the true faith and the lost greatness of a Catholic England, above all, the longing of one who had eaten the bitter bread of exile for almost half his life. In 1581 he had publicly lamented that he and his like 'for our sinnes ... be constrained to spend either al or most of our serviceable yeres out of our natural countrie', and longing for his 'lost fatherland' tolls persistently through his writing. In 1580, as Campion set out for England, he told him that he and his like 'will procure for me and mine the power of returning'.[89]

An autumnal air hangs over Allen's last years as a cardinal. He had an immensely high understanding of his office, as an instrument of the papacy he so much revered: though he was the poorest of the cardinals, he was an active and effective member of the curia, involved in the affairs of Germany, the revision of the Vulgate, the Congregation of the Index.[90] He enjoyed the friendship of, and was treated as an equal by, the greatest men of his age – Borromeo, Bellarmine. He was a man of affairs, keeping open house to English visitors, Catholic or Protestant, in his modest lodgings beside the College, the hub of a network of information, clientage and organization. More than ever he was the central figure in the concerns of the English Catholics, and his eirenical nature and passionate concern for unity were exerted to the full in holding together a community increasingly riven by the bitterness of defeat, in particular the ominous gap opening between the secular clergy and his revered Jesuits.[91] Half-hearted attempts were made by the King of Spain to appoint him Archbishop of Malines, so as to be nearer England, but nothing came of it. And he himself was a disappointed man, aware that there was little chance now of a dramatic restoration of Catholicism, forced to consider seriously the notion, which he had half-heartedly canvassed in the early 1580s, of securing some minimal toleration for Catholics in a Protestant England. In a world in which nobody believed in toleration, it was a project as hopeless as invasion, but we catch a remarkable glimpse of his changed perceptions in the spring and autumn of 1593, through the eyes of an English government go-between, John Arden. Arden, the brother of Allen's Jesuit confessor and closest English friend in Rome, was encouraged by the cardinal to a protracted negotiation for the granting of freedom of conscience to Catholics and a marriage of 'one of Elizabeth's blood' to a Spaniard, to secure the succession. In return, Allen would call off the Pope, the King of Spain and the Catholic League, and all the Catholics would 'do that duty that is due to the Queen, religion excepted, and would take arms in defence of her person and realm against the King of Spain or whosoever'. A striking feature of the whole negotiation was Allen's willingness to shrug off his Spanish involvements. When Arden asked him why he was so keen to unite an English heir with a Spaniard Allen replied that 'he would never wish it if they might have liberty of conscience', and he excused his and other exiles' writings against Elizabeth with 'alas, it was to get favour of the King of Spain who maintained them'. A key to his deepest feelings appeared from an impassioned outburst, when he snatched up a bible and swore 'as I am a priest' that to secure the free practice of Catholicism he would rather 'leave here and all ... and be content to live in prison all the days of my life' in England.[92]

But it would be quite wrong to end on that sombre note. By the time of Allen's death on 16 October 1594 the first heroic phase of the mission was drawing to its close. English Colleges on the Continent were multiplying, and the succession of martyrs would continue – Robert Southwell would go to Tyburn within six months of Allen's death. But the creative verve and the excitement and imaginative power of the mission in the 1580s would never quite be equalled, just as the opportunities which had faced it then were slipping away with the years. The first seminary priests and their Jesuit colleagues, themselves sent to England at Allen's urging, represented one of the most original and most effective experiments of an exceptionally creative and turbulent period of Christian history, and it was Allen's vision they incarnated. No English Protestant attempt to rethink ministry, or to equip men for ministry, was half so radical, or a quarter so professional. No one else in that age conceived so exalted nor so demanding a role for the secular priesthood, and no one else apart from the great religious founders produced a body of men who rose to that ideal so eagerly, and at such cost. The times had demanded invention, decisive action, and he had risen to the challenge. 'The quarrel is God's,' he had told one of his critics, 'and but for Hys holy glory and honor i myght sleepe att ease, and let the worlde wagge and other men worke.'[93] Allen's creation of storm troopers for Counter-Reformation and the energy, humanity and management of men by which he preserved them, showed pastoral resource and vision on a par with that of Cardinal Borromeo in his own generation, or Vincent de Paul in the next. He understood perfectly well what he had achieved, and six months before his death wrote of 'the semynarie of Doway, which is as deere to me as my owne life, and which hath next to God beene the beginning and ground of all the good and salvation which is wrought in England'.[94] Because of him, English Catholicism was given a lifeline to the larger world of Christendom, and a surer, clearer sense of its own identity: because of him, it survived. Elizabethan England produced some really great men, fewer really good ones, and almost none who could be called Europeans. William Allen was all three.

Notes

1. T. F. Knox (ed.), *The Letters and Memorials of William Cardinal Allen*, London, 1882 [hereafter = *Memorials*], pp. xli, 407; T. F. Knox (ed.), *The First and Second Diaries of the English College, Douay*, London, 1878, [hereafter = *D.D.*], pp. 337–8; L. F. Von Pastor, *The History of the Popes*, St Louis, 1930, [hereafter = Pastor], vol. xix, pp. 429–33.
2. *Memorials*, pp. 29–30.
3. *A True, Sincere, and Modest Defense of English Catholics*. 1584, edited by Robert M. Kingdon, Cornell University Press, 1965, p. 127 [hereafter = *Modest Defense*]; *An Apologie and True Declaration of the Institution and endevours of the two English Colleges* ... Henault (Rheims), 1581, p. 12 verso. [hereafter = *Apologie and Declaration*].
4. *Memorials*, pp. 5, 181, 213; 'on Tudor Lancashire and its

religious conservatism', Christopher Haigh, *Reformation and Resistance in Tudor Lancashire*, Cambridge, 1975. For Allen's view of the state of England in the mid 1580s, see Garrett Mattingley, 'William Allen and Catholic Propaganda in England', *Travaux d'Humanisme et Renaissance*, vol. 28, 1957, pp. 325–39.
5. *Memorials* p. 213; *Modest Defense*, p. 56.
6. For the role of the Halls in Tudor Oxford, James McConica, *The History of the University of Oxford*, vol. III, Oxford, 1986, pp. 51–5; Alan B. Coban, *The Medieval English Universities: Oxford and Cambridge to c. 1500*, Scolar Press, 1988, pp. 145–60. They were in effect Colleges within the Colleges, many of them having been annexed to larger institutions, as St Mary's had been acquired by Oriel, though they continued to offer teaching both for the basic Arts course and for further studies in theology and laws.
7. On the course of the Reformation at Oxford, and Martyr's part in it, Jennifer Loach, 'Reformation Controversies' in McConica, *The History of the University of Oxford*, vol. III, pp. 363–74; an unsuccessful attempt was made in 1550 to impose a Protestant head on Allen's own college, Oriel.
8. There is no adequate treatment in English of the Spanish contribution to the Marian restoration: see J. Ignacio Tellechea Idigoras, *Fray Bartolome Carranza vel Cardenal Pole*, Pamplona, 1977, and the same author's *Inglaterra, Flandres y Espana 1557–1559*, Vitoria, 1975. As professor of theology at Dillengen till 1553 De Soto had been a key figure in the German Counter-Reformation; Garcia had been instrumental in securing several of Cranmer's recantations.
9. Loach, op. cit., p. 378.
10. John E. Booty, *John Jewel as Apologist of the Church of England*, London, 1963, p. 63; Michael Richards, 'Thomas Stapleton', *Journal of Ecclesiastical History* vol. XVIII, 1967, pp. 187–99.
11. *Modest Defense*, p. 104.
12. *Modest Defense*, pp. 95, 115.
13. *A Defence and Declaration of the Catholike Churchies Doctrine Touching Purgatory*, Antwerp, 1565, [hereafter *Purgatory*], p. 286.
14. H. N. Bin, *The Elizabethan Religious Settlement*, London, 1907, p. 257.
15. *D.D.*, pp. xxii–xxiii: on the Elizabethan Settlement and its

enforcement in Oxford, Penry Williams, 'Elizabethan Oxford: State, Church and University', in McConica, op. cit., pp. 397–440.
16. Patrick Collinson, *The Birthpangs of Protestant England: Religious and Cultural Change in the Sixteenth and Seventeenth Centuries*, London, 1988, especially p. ix: the case is set out in my *The Stripping of the Altars: Traditional Religion in England 1400–1580*, London and New Haven, 1992, pp. 565–93, and Christopher Haigh, *English Reformations*, Oxford, 1993, pp. 235–50.
17. A sub-committee at the Council of Trent in 1562 considered, and refused, a request that English Catholics should be permitted to attend Book of Common Prayer services, in order to avoid persecution. The ruling, however, was not promulgated formally, and Allen seems not to have known of it: Alexandra Walsham, *Church Papists: Catholicism. Conformity and Confessional Polemic in Early Modern England*, Royal Historical Society Monograph, 1993, pp. 22–3.
18. *D.D.*, pp. xxiii–xxiv; *Memorials*, pp. 56–7.
19. *D.D.*, pp. xxv–xxvi; Manin Haile, *An Elizabethan Cardinal: William Allen*, London, 1914, pp. 57, 67.
20. A. C. Southern, *Elizabethan Recusant Prose 1559–1582*, London, 1950, pp. 517–23: one such publication was *A Notable Discourse. plainelye and truely discussing. who are the right Ministers of the Catholike Church*, Douai, 1575.
21. For the Jewel controversy, Southern, *Recusant Prose*, pp. 59–118 (Allen's contributions discussed in detail pp. 103–9); Booty, *Jewel*, pp. 58–82; Peter Milward, *Religious Controversies of the Elizabethan Age*, London, 1978, pp. 1–16.
22. *Purgatory*, pp. 37 verso, 282–3.
23. *Purgatory*, p. 12 verso; Southern, *Recusant Prose*, p. 109.
24. John Bossy, *The English Catholic Community 1570–1850*, London, 1975, p. 13, quoting A. L. Rowse, *The England of Elizabeth*, London, 1951, p. 461. For a critique of this general view, and an assertion of Allen's 'keen intelligence', see Mattingley, 'William Allen and Catholic Propaganda', pp. 335–6.
25. C. S. Lewis, *English Literature in the Sixteenth Century*, Oxford, 1954, pp. 438–41.
26. *Purgatory*, pp. 132–3.
27. Loach, in McConica, op. cit., p. 386; Peter Guilday, *The English Catholic Refugees on the Continent 1558–1795*, London,

1914, pp. 1–27, 63–65; Southern, *Recusant Prose*, pp. 14–30; John Bossy, *English Catholic Community*, pp. 12–14.
28. J. H. Pollen (ed.), *Memoirs of Robert Parsons, S.J.*, Catholic Record Society, vol. ii, Miscellanea, 1906, p. 62.
29. *Apologie and Declaration*, p. 19.
30. By far the most stimulating and valuable modern account is that in Bossy, op. cit., pp. 14–18 to which I am greatly indebted though, as will be seen, I dissent from some of his central contentions. A cruder and somewhat facile statement of a similar view to Bossy's will be found in J. C. H. Aveling, *The Handle and the Axe*, London, 1976, pp. 53–6.
31. D.D., p. xxviii: *Memorials*, p. 22.
32. Bossy, *English Catholic Community*, p. 15.
33. P. Renold (ed.), *Letters of William Allen and Richard Barret 1572–1598*, Catholic Record Society, 1967, pp. 4–5 [hereafter = *Letters*]. The allusion is to St Luke ch. 9 verses 52–3, Vulgate version.
34. P. Ryan (ed.), 'Correspondence of Cardinal Allen' in Catholic Record Society, *Miscellanea VII*, 1911, pp. 47–63, quotation p. 63 [hereafter = 'Correspondence'].
35. J. H. Pollen, *The English Catholics in the Reign of Queen Elizabeth*, London, 1920, p. 247.
36. *A Treatise Made in Defence of the lauful power and authoritie of Priesthood to remitte sinnes*, Louvain, 1567, preface (unpaginated). He is actually quoting from St Basil, but makes the application to England and 'our new ministers' explicit.
37. *Memorials*, p. 367.
38. He and Allen took their doctorates in Divinity together in 1571.
39. D.D., pp. xxvii–xxxi; *Letters*, pp. 8–11.
40. Patrick McGrath and Joy Rowe, 'Anstruther Analysed: the Elizabethan Seminary Priests', *Recusant History*, vol. 18, 1986, pp. 1–13.
41. *Apologie*, p. 22 verso; 'Correspondence' pp. 66–67.
42. Printed in Richard Simpson, *Edmund Campion*, London, 1896, pp. 509–13.
43. D.D., p. xxxviii; *Memorials*, pp. 61–2.
44. For a good account of which see T. Deutscher, 'Seminaries and the Education of Novarese Parish Priests, 1593–1627', *Journal of Ecclesiastical History*, vol. 32, pp. 303–19.
45. Allen's own account of the syllabus is in *Memorials*, pp. 62–7,

translated *D.D.*, pp. xxxviii–xliii: it is helpfully expanded by Gregory Martin in *Roma Sancta* (G. B. Parks, ed.), Roma, 1969, pp. 4–9: the cases of conscience devised for the College are edited by P. J. Holmes, *Elizabethan Casuistry*, Catholic Record Society, 1981.
46. *D.D.*, pp. xxxix.
47. *Memorials*, pp. 32–3.
48. *D.D.*, p. x xxi–xxxii: Godfrey Anstruther, *The Seminary Priests*, vol. I, Ware and Durham, 1968, p. 224.
49. *Memorials*, p. 17.
50. *Apologie*, pp. 67–8.
51. *Memorials*, p. 33.
52. *Letters*, pp. 131–4; *Memorials*, p. 344.
53. *Memorials*, p. 36.
54. *Apologie*, pp. 109 verso–110: for Allen's own account of his advice on martyrdom to Campion, *A Briefe Historie of the Glorious Martyrdom of XII Reverend Priests*, 1582, sig. d iii verso: for the comment to Fr Aggazari, see the preface to J. H. Pollen's edition of the *Briefe Historie*, p. ix; *Memorials*, p. 135.
55. *Apologie*, pp. 117, verso 118.
56. *D.D.*, p. xliii: *Memorials*, p. 67.
57. *Memorials*, p. 35.
58. Walsham, *Church Papists*, pp. 22–49.
59. *Memorials*, p. 34; see Walsham, *Church Papists*, pp. 62–3, though I think that Ms Walsham interprets Allen's text more permissively than he intended.
60. *Letters*, pp. 30–3.
61. *Memorials*, p. 354.
62. *Letters*, pp. 194–5.
63. *D.D.*, pp. li–lvi.
64. On the Bull in general, and Catholic opinion about it, A. O. Meyer, *England and the Catholic Church under Queen Elizabeth*, London, 1916, pp. 37 ff., 52–5, 76–90, 138–41; T. H. Clancy, *Papist Pamphleteers*, Chicago, 1964, pp. 46–49.
65. *Apologie*, p. 17.
66. *Letters*, pp. 276–84; *Modest Defense*, pp. 146–214.
67. Anthony Kenny, 'From Hospice to College 1559–1579', *The Venerabile*, vol. 121, 1962 (Sexcentenary Issue), pp. 228–9.
68. *Letters*, pp. 284–92; Pollen, *The English Catholics in the Reign of Queen Elizabeth*, London, 1920, pp. 197–200.
69. *Memorials*, p. 38.

70. *Memorials*, p. 131; *Letters*, p. 75.
71. *Memorials*, pp. 217–8; Philip Hughes, *The Reformation in England*, vol. III, London, 1954, pp. 297–300.
72. *Memorials*, p. 233; Mattingley, 'William Allen', p. 333.
73. Mattingley, 'William Allen', p. 332.
74. The most extended treatment of Allen's political involvement at this time is Knox's introduction to *Memorials*, pp. li–lxxi.
75. *Letters*, pp. 156–66: the memorial for the Pope was identified and edited by Garret Mattingley, *loc cit*. The reference to the 'promiscuous multitude' comes from *Memorials*, p. lxvii.
76. For one which see *Memorials*, pp. c–ci.
77. *Memorials*, pp. cvi–viii.
78. *Memorials*, p. cxi.
79. See especially *Modest Defense*, pp. 124–6: *A Briefe Historie of the Glorious Martyrdom of XII Reverend Priests*, Preface to the Reader, sig. c. ii.
80. The evidence is assembled by Mattingley, loc cit., pp. 336–7.
81. See, for example, 'Correspondence', p. 45, recommending Thomas Stapleton as a potentially valuable member of the invasion fleet of 1576 'but he knows nothing at all about the enterprise'.
82. *Modest Defense*, p. 196.
83. *Modest Defense*, p. 141; T. H. Clancy, *Papist Pamphleteers*, Chicago, 1964, p. 51.
84. *The Copie of a Letter Written by M. Doctor Allen: concerning the yeelding up of the Citie of Daventrie, unto his Catholike Maiestie*, by Sir William Stanley, Antwerp, 1587, pp. 17, 29.
85. *An Admonition to the Nobility and People of England ... mode for the execution of his Holines Sentence, by the highe and mightie Kinge Catholike of Spain. By the Cardinal of Englande*, 1588.
86. *Modest Defense*, p. 224.
87. *Admonition to the Nobilitie*, sig. D5.
88. *Apologie*, p. 4 verso.
89. *Apologie*, p. 7; Simpson, *Campion*, p. 134.
90. Pastor vol. 21, p. 250; vol. 22, p. 391; vol. 23, p. 311.
91. See, for example, his letter to John Mush in March 1594, *Memorials*, pp. 357–8.
92. R. B. Wemham (ed.), *Lists and Analyses of State Papers Foreign Series Elizabeth I*, London, HMSO, vol. i, 1964, no. 627; vol. iv, 1984, nos. 638–43; vol. v, 1989, no. 627: and see the remark-

able letter to Richard Hopkins, August 14 1593, *Memorials*, pp. 348–51, about just such a 'reasonable toleration' – 'I thank God I am not estranged from the place of my birth most sweet, nor so affected to foreigners that I prefer not the weal of that people above all mortal things'.
93. *Memorials*, p. 37.
94. *Memorials*, p. 358.

This article, which appeared in the 1995 edition of 'The Venerabile', was originally given as a talk in the College church on 17 October 1994 during the 400th Anniversary Celebrations of Cardinal Allen's death.

One of the frescoes in the English College Tribune, originally painted by Pomerancio. It shows the rather fanciful spectacle of St John Fisher, St Thomas More and Blessed Margaret Pole together on the scaffold. These paintings, dating from 1583, are important evidence for the early veneration of the English Martyrs.

The English College and the Martyrs' Cause

Bishop Brian Foley

The English College has close links with the Cause of the martyrs, and this is best illustrated by the pictures of Nicolo Circignani, called after his birthplace *Il Pomerancio*, in the College church, for these paintings and the book of engravings by Cavallieri were the decisive factor in the first beatifications of 1886.

Various suggestions have been given for the existence of the paintings. It has been said that they were the result of the enthusiasm engendered by the Holy Year of 1575, or by the discovery of the supposed tomb of St Lawrence in the cemetery of Ciriaca when the Via Tiburtina was being widened a little later. The origin of the paintings was, however, due to other causes.

The newly-formed Society of Jesus had been discussing and experimenting with new didactic methods and in particular with what we should call 'visual aids'. In its General Congregation of 1558 new rulings had been set out for the decoration of their churches and residences, and also for the illustrating of texts for novices and students. With regard to churches and chapels, it was recommended that instead of the aesthetic wall paintings of the past there should be painted sets or series of pictures depicting sequences of episodes and annotated with texts from Scripture and elsewhere of an explanatory kind. These 'lettered *testimoni*' were to be in Latin and Italian. Michele Lauretano, later Rector of the German College, brought out an influential *Discorso intorno alle immagini* and when he died it was written of him: 'Fu il primo ... che cominciasse a far dipingere nelle chiese li Martirii ... con le sue note che dichiarono le persone e le qualità dei tormenti, come si vede in S. Stefano Rotondo; e dopo fu seguitato da molti altri'.[1]

With regard to books of study, the Spanish Rector of the *Collegio Romano*, Jerome Nadal (1564–7), printed illustrated texts of gospel narratives with captions and he and other professors of the time encouraged students to illustrate their note and text books themselves.[2] Some writers have seen in these new methods the influence of the *Spiritual Exercises* and the concept of 'composition of place'. The Council of Trent, at a time when it was much influenced by the new Jesuit theologians, gave approval in its decrees of 1563 to didactic wall paintings in churches providing that they had 'clarity, truthfulness and usefulness'.[3]

The first church erected by the Jesuits in Rome was the *Annuntiata* (or *Annuntiatella*). It was on the site given for the *Collegio Romano* and was destined for the chapel of the College.[4] It was built entirely by the labour of the fathers and brothers and here for the first time they were able to put their ideas into effect. The *Annuntiata* was opened in 1567 and remained the College chapel until the 1620s when S. Ignazio was built. Its entrance was in what is now Via di S. Ignazio roughly beneath the arch which joins S. Ignazio to the *Biblioteca Casanatense*. This small church was that in which the first sodalists of the *Prima Primaria* (including St Stanislaus Kostka, St Aloysius Gonzaga, St John Berchmans and some of our own martyrs) had gathered for meetings and prayer. It was, therefore, dear to the Society, and when the great church of S. Ignazio was being built, an effort was made to preserve what could be saved of the old *Annuntiata*. The left aisle had to go to make way for the new church, but part of the nave was saved and some of the apse incorporated into the new building, while most of the right aisle was preserved.

It is still possible with some difficulty to visit these parts of the old chapel. Anyone wishing to see the remaining part of the nave and apse should make his way through a door to the right of the sanctuary of S. Ignazio, where he will find himself in the *cereria* or *gardaroba* used by the sacristan lay brothers. These brothers discourage entrance, but if one can prove devotion to the early saints of the Society and interest in the *Prima Primaria* he will be permitted to peep into this part of the old *Annuntiata*. To gain admittance to the right aisle is more difficult. Access is through the great doorway in the Piazza del Collegio Romano where a number of officials are on guard in what is now a large Secondary School. However, it is possible to persuade them to escort you through the left colonnade where, at the top, a small opening gives access into the right aisle of the old chapel. There are now no traces remaining of the frescoes with which Federico Zucchari covered the walls; there are, however, in the sacristy of S. Ignazio examples of his work and that of others who assisted him. Apart from the recreation room of the noviciate at Sant' Andrea, which is known to have been covered by very early picture-paintings, these frescoes were the first didactic paintings on which the Jesuits embarked.[5]

After this the fathers began to look round for an artist who would make his own their ideas and embody them on the walls of their college chapels and churches. It may seem strange that they should have wished to concentrate on these chapels rather than on their great church of the *Gesù*. Writers seem to agree that in the latter part of the sixteenth century there were few really good artists to decorate the great new churches of the newly-founded orders such as the *Chiesa Nuova* (Oratorians), S. Andrea della Valle (Theatines) and the *Gesù* (Jesuits). It was not for that reason, however, that the Society of Jesus made its priority the decorating with 'annotated pictures' the chapels of their colleges. Their main concern was for the training of their students and novices for the dangerous missions ahead. They wanted to place before them not works of art but brutally realistic pictures of dangers to be encountered and even torments to be endured.[6]

When looking for the artist they required, their attention was directed to Circignani (not to be confused with his son Antonio and Cristofero Roncalli, also called 'Il Pomerancio'). This artist had worked briefly in Rome in 1564–5 and had been noticed by Vasari in his *Lives* of 1568 as a *'pittore giovane'* who had done good work in the *Duomo* of Orvieto. He had been invited back to Rome to do important work for Pope Gregory XIII being given charge of the third *piano* of that Pope's loggias. He was persuaded to work for the Society and assigned by the fathers to begin at Sant' Apollinare.

The church of S. Apollinare had been given by Pope Julius III to St Ignatius. Later it was made over to the German College, which the saint began to set up and give Constitutions, though it was not officially founded until 1573. The *Germanicum* was to possess S. Apollinare as its home for more than two hundred years. In 1581 its Rector was Fr Lauretani (mentioned above) and he set Circignani to paint a cycle of thirteen *quadri* in the tribune of the church depicting the life and death of the patron saint. He did this in the 'manieristic idiom' required, which he made his own. Appropriate texts and captions or 'lettered annotations' were provided by the fathers and not only the tribune but other parts of the church also came to be covered in the same manner. The old church of Sant' Apollinare was demolished in the time of Benedict XIV (1740–58) and so those old paintings have been lost.[7] The German College still possesses books of receipts for payments of these pictures and the diary of Fr Lauretano referring to them. A book of etchings or engravings of these pictures was brought out by J. B. Cavallieri entitled *Beati Apollinaris martyris ... Nicolao Circiniano depictae visuntur, Romae,* 1586.[8]

After he had finished his work at S. Apollinare, Circignani was set to work by the Jesuits at Santo Stefano Rotondo. This had come into their possession in this way. Pope Gregory XIII in 1579 had set up a Hungarian College and presented it with the church and annexed buildings of S. Stefano. The new college, however, did not prosper; it never attracted more than four students.[9] The Pope decided to amalgamate it with the German College and it became, what it has remained ever since, the German–Hungarian College. The staff and students do not seem ever to have resided there. They used it rather as a day centre (as the English College used La Magliana and the vineyard at the foot of the Palatine near S. Gregorio). The Germans found S. Stefano in a ruinous condition but were able to install Circignani there in 1582. He was given the commission to depict as graphically as he could the sufferings of the ancient martyrs of the late Roman Empire. He was to do this in thirty-one pictures in the *ambulacro* beginning as always with the Crucifixion and its single text. This was a vast enterprise covering a hundred and thirty-seven episodes with a multitude of figures and examples of martyrdom.[10]

The artist devoted five months to this 'pictorial martyrology', leaving the landscapes and background to Matteo da Siena and others, who also filled in the explanatory captions and texts. The painter Tempesta also did much other work in S. Stefano. Mancini wrote of Pomerancio and his work here: '*Fu huomo di grande invenzione e prestezza come si vede in S. Stefano Rotondo, che dicono che tutte quelle pitture fece in un estate facendone un quadro il giorno*'.[11] These paintings at S. Stefano were not intended to be artistic and they will strike the modern viewer as insensitive in the extreme, almost exaggerating the cruelty of the executioners. What had been demanded of him was that they should move not to admiration but emulation. Contemporaries approved of them. We read of Pope Sixtus V '*fu visto nell' ammirare quei spettacoli lacrimare*'.[12] We also are told: '*Circa l'istesso tempo il Cardinale Farnese ando a vedere S. Stefano e vidde tutte le pitture e ne resto molto contento*'.[13] The artist had completed his work at S. Stefano by the end of September 1582. A book of engravings of the pictures was produced, a copy of which is in the College archives. It must have been presented to Cardinal Allen having on it the dedication of the author (Julius Rosciush): *'Ad Alanum virum religio (sissimum) doctissm Cardinalem creatum vii sectil MDXXCVII'*.[14]

Having finished his work at S. Stefano, Circignani was next employed by the Jesuits at the English College in 1583. He was commissioned to do a similar set of paintings of martyrdoms to those at S. Apollinare and S. Stefano except that they were to depict ancient and modern martyrdoms in England and Wales. The Rector at the time was Fr Alfonso Agazzari, S.J., and he wrote a long letter about this project and others concerning the College to the General on 13 October 1583. A great part of the letter is taken up with an account of George Gilbert the young Englishman who made himself responsible for defraying the cost. Here is a part of the letter:

> Very Rev. Father in Christ,
> ... among the saints (Gilbert) showed a great veneration for the martyrs. ... The holy youth took great pains to learn the names of all the English martyrs of former and modern times, and caused their acts to be represented in paintings with which he adorned the whole church of the College placing also the holy confessors alternatively with the martyrs over the capitals of the columns. This cost him seven hundred *scudi*, having collected for this purpose contributions from several of his English friends. He used to say that his object was not only to honour these glorious martyrs and to manifest before the world the glory and splendour of the Church in England but that the students of the college, beholding the example of their predecessors might stimulate themselves to follow it. ...
>
> Alfonso Agazzari.
>
> Rome, English College,
> October 14, 1583[15]

The actual date of the paintings was indeed that year of 1583 and not, as sometimes stated, earlier or later. The *Annual Letters* of the English College, 1583, report that 'the College is now beautifully decorated'.

George Gilbert was born of a Suffolk Calvinist family of high fortune and position, which he inherited when young. While travelling on the Continent with royal licence he was received into the Church by Fr Robert Parsons, S.J., in 1579. On his return to England he was a co-founder of what was called 'The Young Mens Catholic Association'. This was composed of young nobles and gentlemen of property who 'pledged to content themselves with the bare necessities of their state and to bestow the rest for the good of the Catholic cause'. This Association was solemnly blessed by Pope Gregory XIII in April, 1580. Its activities soon were known and being monitored by the authorities, and Gilbert was advised to return to the Continent. He stayed a short while with Allen at Douai, who later described him as '*summus patrum presbyterorum patronus*'. Proceeding to Rome, he entered the English College but whether with a view to the priesthood or in some other capacity is not clear. He did not take the College oath. The Pope frequently used him and he was asked to go on a papal mission to France when he died in the College, being admitted to the Society of Jesus on his deathbed in 1583.[16]

Gilbert left the choice and supervision of the Pomerancio paintings in the College chapel to Fr William Good, S.J., the spiritual director; he was a Marian priest who became a Jesuit in 1577 and was now too old to be sent to England. The College series of paintings is comparable to that at S. Stefano. It contained thirty-nine *quadri*, having the same kind of captions, texts and explanatory notes as the artist's earlier series at S. Apollinare and S. Stefano. The subjects ranged from the sending of St Joseph of Arimathea to England to the martyrdoms of SS Alban, Boniface and Thomas of Canterbury. The Reformation martyrs commence with the Carthusians and proceed to other religious, priests and laypeople, who had suffered up to 1583; these included the three recently martyred *alumni* of the College. The pictures, as can be seen from the present copies in the Tribune, follow the now accustomed 'manneristic realism' inspired by the Jesuit teaching ideas of the times.

This series in the College chapel was the last painted by Pomerancio of its kind for the Jesuit Fathers. He continued to work for them with single projects but did not again for them depict a *series* of martyr or other episodes. The years 1584–5 find him painting a series at S. Giovanni dei Fiorentini (the church of which St Philip Neri had been rector until 1575). The series of pictures he painted there were much more delicate; they were *Storielli della vita di S. Francesco*. He soon began working in a number of Rome's churches such as S. Maria di Loreto, S. Pudentiana, SS Giovanni e Paolo, Santa Croce and the *Gesù*, where he worked in the first two chapels on the left. The last church he worked in, before he left Rome in 1589 for *Citta della Pieve,* was S. Lorenzo in Damaso.[17]

Towards the end of the 1590s the Jesuits were presented by the Pope with the church of San Vitale. It is difficult to realize today that this church in fact is quite near S. Andrea al Quirinale where they had the Noviciate. It was possible to walk entirely through vineyards and orchards from one to the other and San Vitale was described at that time to be *'in piena campagna'*. It was, therefore, an ideal arrangement to unite the two churches together for the use of the novices.[18] The Jesuits proceeded to decorate San Vitale with a series of martyr paintings like those they had previously commissioned from Pomerancio. They now used the services of an artist called Fiammeri who entered the Society as a laybrother. Fr General Aquaviva himself supervised this series of paintings which may still be seen at San Vitale. His letters are said to show his interest and that he wanted something for his novices similar to the series previously done but less harsh and insensitive.[19] These pictures at San Vitale (the church allocated to St John Fisher as his titular) make an interesting study. They, too, have martyrdom as their central theme, but it is only by looking at them closely and studying the captions and texts that this becomes apparent. At first glance one is struck by the idyllic pastoral scenes so delicately depicted that some of them have been mistakenly attributed to Poussin. The martyrs are introduced unobtrusively, unlike those in the Pomerancio paintings.[20]

The last decade of Circignani's life was spent at *Citta della Pieve*, where he had acquired property. He was made a *'cittadino onorario della cittadinanza umbra'*. In 1594 he was invited back to Rome to address the *Accademia di San. Luca* to which he had been elected in 1581. He must have died by 1599 for in that year his *'vedova Teodora'* is found administering his property.[21] Little can be gleaned of his character but the following description was given of him: *'vestiva con semplicità toscana ... net parlare pareva essere semplice e certo non colto ... pero era arguto e sapeva ii fat to suo'*.[22]

What of Circignani's merit as an artist? He has been mocked and vilified for his series of martyr paintings. Augustus Hare spoke of him at S. Stefano as 'contemptible and brutalising' and calls him that 'pretentious dauber'. This is less than just and is to ignore his brief for them, and the other work that he did. His Jesuit patrons had given him a particular commission and expected of him that 'clarity, truth, and usefulness' called for in the Tridentine decrees. Much of his other work is quite fine and even tender in its delicacy. Some of it, like his paintings in the *Torre dei Venti* in the Vatican, has been even extravagantly praised.[23] Like other artists he had to be a painter of *'due pennelli'* in accordance with the brief given to him. Fr Lauretano, who may be said to have been the creator of that peculiar style of painting, applauded Circignani's work for him calling him *'il maestro del genere'* though admitting that some of what he produced was *'mediocremente buono'*. It was his merit to make his own that *'stilo controriformistico di immediata ispirizaione gesuitica'* and to have that style named after him and copied until the middle of the eighteenth century. What, however, was most important for us was that he carried out faithfully in the College chapel the commission entrusted to him by Gilbert and Frs Agazzari and Good, S.J. thus enabling the martyrs' Cause to reach its first fulfilment in 1886.

There had been previous attempts made to beatify the martyrs. In the archives of Propaganda Fide there is the list of martyrs compiled and sent by Bishop Richard Smith in 1628 and called after him the *'Chalcedon Catalogue'*.[24] It was hoped that this would swiftly bring about honours being paid liturgically to our martyrs. It was indeed followed in 1643 by a decree of Urban VIII authorizing the setting up of an *Ordinary Process* by the Archbishop of Cambrai (assisted by the Bishops of St Omer and Ypres). These attempts failed because of 'the calamity of the times'.[25] Several attempts were made after the restoration of the hierarchy to procure a feast of the martyrs. The Holy See insisted each time, when requests were made, that there must be an *Ordinary Process*, which was finally set up in Westminster and was taking its long course when events took a dramatic turn, attention being drawn to the Pomerancio paintings and the book of Cavallieri engravings. What transpired is shown in the following letter sent by Mgr Henry O'Callaghan, the College Rector and acting as joint Vice-Postulator for the Cause to the Secretary of Cardinal Manning:

Rome, June 5, 1886
... please tell the Cardinal with my respectful regards that I have had the consolation of helping on very materially the Cause of the English Martyrs by submitting for more careful examination the book of engravings published at Rome in 1584 representing the paintings in the church. Yesterday I had a long interview with Mgr Caprara (the Promoter) who spoke of the book as *un documento grave* as it was published *cum privilegio Gregorii XIII*. He therefore said that he must reconsider his course and see whether it would not be advisable to propose at once some for beatification.[26]

As he had promised, the Promoter immediately took up the matter, expressing to the Congregation that the book of engravings of Cavallieri afforded proof of ecclesiastical *cultus* accorded by the Pope to fifty-four martyrs. The Congregation accepted this at its sitting on 4 December 1886, and voted that the martyrs there exhibited were worthy of 'equipollent' or equivalent beatification. The Congregation then passed two resolutions to be sent to the Holy Father, the one that the Cause be officially introduced, and the other that these martyrs should be beatified. The Holy Father accepted these resolutions and on the feast of St Thomas of Canterbury, 29 December 1886, in the Decree *Anglia Sanctorum Insula*, the cult of the fifty-four martyrs was confirmed, that is they were beatified *'equipollenter'*.

The *Decree of Beatification* states:-

1. Pope Gregory XIII granted in honour of these English martyrs several ecclesiastical privileges appertaining to public ecclesiastical worship, and especially that of using their relics in the consecration of altars where relics of ancient martyrs were not available.

2. The same Pope after he had caused the sufferings of the Christian martyrs of old to be painted in fresco by Nicholas Circignani in the church of St Stephen on the Coelian Hill, permitted also the martyrs of England both of ancient and modern times, and including those who died between 1535 and 1583 under Henry VIII and Elizabeth I, to be likewise represented by the same artist in the chapel of the English College in Rome, along with canonised saints, such as St Thomas of Canterbury. These representations remained, with the knowledge and approbation of the Roman Pontiffs, for two centuries. Although they were destroyed at the end of the eighteenth century, fortunately a book of engravings which preserved the representations in the frescoes had been published by permission of Gregory XIII in

1584, and from this record the names of fifty-four martyrs could be discovered, either from the inscriptions or from other indications. (There then follow the names of the fifty-four martyrs.)[27]

The College, then, through its martyr paintings of Pomerancio and their engravings by Cavallieri, given by George Gilbert and supervised by Frs Agazzari and Good, S.J., was responsible for the evidence needed for the initial beatifications. In later times it was members of the College such as Christopher Grene (the 'archivist' of the Cause) and John Morris (the 'apostle' of the Cause) who kept the impetus going. May the College ever have among its *alumni* those who will continue to foster the Cause of our martyrs and who will take pride in bearing the Roman's proudest title: *cultor martyrum*.

Postscript

After finishing the above I have noticed another set of martyr paintings of Circignani of uncertain date but after his series at S. Apollinare, S. Stefano, and the English College. They are described by Baglione as *'ciclo con diverse storie dei martyri nel choro dietro l'altar maggiore a S. Cecilia distrutto senza che se ne serbasse traccia'* (Cf Mara Nimmo, op. cit. and G. Baglione, *Le vite dei Pittori etc.*, Accademia dei Lincei, cura Mariani, Roma, 1935.)

Notes

1. *Necrologia del P. Michele Lauretano*, 16 Agosto, 1610, in Arch. S.J. Casa Gener., MSS 185, f.25; cited in P. Haskell, *Patrons and Painters*, 67, London, 1963.
2. L. H. Monssen, 'A Contribution to Jesuit Iconography', in *The Art Bulletin*, vol. 43, 133 (Quarterly of the College Art Association of America).

3. Ibid., p. 130. Cf. also Mara Nimmo, 'L'Eta perfetta della virilita di Nicolo Circignani dale Pomerancie', *Studi Romani*, Luglio–Decembre, 1984, p. 202.
4. E. Rinaldi, *La Fondazione del Collegio Romano*, pp. 29–45, Arezzo, 1914. Cf. also G. Martinelli, S. Ignazio, 21 seq., Roma, 1967 (N. 97 of *Le Chiese di Roma Illust*).
5. L. H. Monssen, 131.
6. P. Haskell, pp. 60–68.
7. M. Armellini, *Chiese di Roma*, 2 ediz., reprinted 1985, pp. 345–7.
8. Mara Nimmo, 203 who has studied the receipts paid for Circignani's work in Arch. del Collo Germo citing *Libro Mastro B. 1580–3*, c. 44 and 91. Cf. also L. H. Monssen, p. 131.
9. Florio Banfi, 'La Chiesa di Santo Stefano e Il Monastero etc.', *Capitolium*, XXVIII, 1953, pp. 289–300. Cf. also C. Ceschi, *Memorie di S. Stefane Rotondo*, pp. 161–9.
10. Ibid.
11. H. L. Monssen, p. 132, where this quotation of Mancini (d. 1610) is cited in his *Considerazioni pittura*. Cf. also Mara Nimmo, p. 201.
12. Cf. Florio Banfi, p. 297.
13. H. L. Monssen, p. 132, where the *Diary of P. Michele Lauretano* for November 1582 is cited; he was Rector of the German College 1573–1587. Cf. also Mara Nimmo, p. 202.
14. This copy is entitled *Triumphus Martyrum in Templo D. Stephani Coeli Montis Expressus*. It is a later edition, the first being *Ecclesiae Militantis Triumphus* etc., 1583.
15. H. Foley, S.J., *Records of the English Province of the Society of Jesus*, vol. III, pp. 687–8, Manresa, 1878.
16. Ibid. pp. 658–704 for full account of Geo. Gilbert. Cf. also Bartoli, *Della Istoria della Compagnia di Gesu, L'Inghilterra*, for extended account. Also DNB.
17. Cf. N. Circignani, *Dizionario Biogr. Degli Italiani*, vol. 25; pp. 775–8.
18. L. Huetter e Vincenzo Golzio, 'San Vitale', *Le Chiese di Roma Illustr.*, N. 35, 17.
19. F. Haskell, p. 67.
20. Ibid.
21. N. Circignani, *Dizionario degli Italiani*, vol. 25, p. 778.
22. Mara Nimmo, p. 209.

23. Ibid., p. 198, where the Dominican Ignazio Danti is quoted as speaking of some *'ex picturis elegantissimis Nicolai Circignani quibus turricula Ventorum undique exornatur'*.
24. Arch. Prop. Fide, SOCG, 347, ff. 590–615; copy in Westminster Archives.
25. *Bullarium Romanum*, Torino, 1869, p. 246; *Summarium* 11, pp. 43–8. A draft of the Brief is in Vat. Arch. Secret. Brev. 918, ff. 44r–49v.
26. J. H. Pollen, S.J., *The Life and Letters of Fr John Morris*, pp. 212–3, London, 1896.
27. The title of the *Book of Engravings* of the Pomerancio paintings in the English College which gave rise to the first beatifications is: *Ecclesiae Anglicanae Trophaea siue Sanctorum Martyrum qui pro Christo mortem in Anglia subierunt etc. per Jo. Bap. de Caualleriys aeneis typis repraesentantur, Romae, 1584.*

This article first appeared in the 1987 edition of 'The Venerabile', which celebrated the Beatification of eighty-five English Martyrs on 22 November that year. Nine of these new beati were former students of the English College.

Cardinal Philip Howard.

Cardinal Philip Howard, Rome and English Recusancy

Judith F. Champ

Philip Howard remains an enigmatic character – clearly influential in Church and State in his time – but a shadowy figure in the history of English Recusancy. Yet his career opens a window on all the major problems which dogged the English Catholics in the seventeenth century – Episcopal government, relations between religious and secular clergy, loyalty to the Stuarts, the ramifications of the Oates plot and, of course, finance. He played a crucial role in the most turbulent period of Recusancy between the Restoration and the Revolution Settlement, yet because he spent the last six months of his life destroying papers his influence is not easy to assess.

Howard was the subject of a lengthy unpublished biography by his later confrère Father Godfrey Anstruther, O.P. This was a project which began in 1955 when Anstruther was living at Santa Sabina in Rome and was Spiritual Director at the Venerable English College. He wrote to a friend, '... I have been rereading Palmer's *Life of Howard*,[1] and I never realized before how uninspired it is. It has all the matter but no literary merit and, alas, no references. Shall we do a new one?'[2] His new one occupied much of the rest of his life and it was a source of frustration that he was never able to get it published. This paper draws heavily upon it and I am grateful for the late Father Anstruther's exhaustive research and to Father Bede Bailey, O.P. for access to his files at the Dominican Archives in Edinburgh.

Philip Howard's early biography is easily told. He was the great-grandson and namesake of St Philip Howard who died in the Tower in 1589 and grandson of the art collector Earl Thomas Howard who trawled Italy with Inigo Jones in the early 17th century. Philip was brought up in the Church of England, but did his Grand Tour in the company of his grandfather and encountered his Catholic grandmother in Antwerp. Her influence and that of a Dominican, Father John Baptist Hackett, introduced the young Howard to the practice of Catholicism. Despite fierce opposition from the rest of his family, not only was Philip Howard received into the Church but clothed as a Dominican friar. The earl did all in his power to prevent this, including accusations of undue influence and gaining the notice of Barberini the Cardinal Protector of England, and the Pope himself. Despite the ferocious and constant efforts of his family, Howard was professed as a Dominican in San Clemente in Rome in October 1646 and ordained priest at Rennes in 1652. The first part of his adult life was devoted to the Order to which he was committed and to the revival of its English Province. His greatest achievement in this respect was the founding of a house at Bornhem in Flanders for English Friars and a convent for the Second Order nuns eventually settled in Brussels. Much of his time was spent crisscrossing the channel, raising funds and encouraging the new foundation of which he was made Prior. In 1660 he was made Vicar General of the English Province of the Order.

Soon after the Restoration and the marriage of Charles II to Catherine of Braganza, Philip Howard began the public career in England which was to draw away much of his time and attention from the Order. His uncle Lord

Aubigny was responsible for the Catholic ceremonial of the royal marriage and Howard was the only English witness at the private ceremony. As a result he was appointed as the Queen's chaplain and took up a career at Court from 1662. This did not prevent his continued interest in his Order and as early as 1663 he was investigating the formation of another Friary in France. He continued to function as Prior of Bornhem.

Obviously, Philip Howard became known at Court as something of a public figure, especially after succeeding his uncle as Grand Almoner to the Queen in 1665. This post gave him charge over her oratory at Whitehall and a state salary. Pepys, on a visit to Court in 1666 described him as a 'good natured gentleman' with whom he 'talked merrily of the differences of our religion'.

The Restoration raised again possibilities for the English Catholics of an environment in which ecclesiastical administration might be regularized. The first half of the seventeenth century had seen the Recusant communities riven by rivalries and disputes over who should exercise oversight after the loss of the hierarchy. In the 1620s William Bishop and Richard Smith had been appointed as Vicars Apostolic and England was placed under the care of the newly formulated Congregation of Propaganda Fide. The Vicariate effectively lasted only until Smith went into exile in 1631, after which there was no bishop in England. The eponymous Bishop William Bishop lived only nine months after his arrival in England in July 1623 but his only significant governmental act was to have ramifications long after. He instituted a Chapter of twenty canons to advise him and preserve jurisdiction in case of his death. The Chapter was *de facto* recognized by Propaganda, but the formal Bull of erection of the Chapter was never given. Richard Smith not only continued it, but gave it the right to elect its own canons and dean if the Vicariate was vacant. Smith tried to exercise jurisdiction from France, but the unconfirmed Chapter took on greater significance and after his death in 1655 it assumed jurisdiction over the Church of England. At no point did Rome ever grant it formal status and jurisdiction, which created ticklish problems over clerical appointments and faculties.

The Chapter pressed, not only for its own formal recognition, but for the appointment of a Bishop in Ordinary, not a Vicar Apostolic, to succeed Smith. A Bishop would be expected to work closely with a Chapter; a Vicar Apostolic could in theory override what was essentially an uncanonical body.

Howard became drawn into this delicate problem when in 1668 John Leyburn, the new secretary to the Chapter suggested to his fellow canons that Howard be their nomination as Bishop. The London members who knew him were enthusiastic but others were less so, for the reason that they were lukewarm about a religious in control of secular clergy. Thus Howard was dragged into the perennial bitter secular v regular wrangle, although he had the virtue in some eyes of at least not being a Jesuit. However, the Internuncio of Brussels, on whom Rome largely depended for reliable information on England, knew Howard well through his Dominican foundations and commended him to the Pope for the appointment. The matter was virtually settled by mid-1670 and it was confirmed by a 'particular congregation' in September of that year that Howard would be appointed Vicar Apostolic for England and Scotland. According to Anstruther there was 'no serious doubt outside the Chapter that he was to be a Vicar Apostolic and not a Bishop'.[3] Bossy shared this view that no one seriously thought that they would get ordinaries.[4]

In April 1672 Howard was secretly appointed titular Bishop of Helenopolis, with a view to taking up the post as Vicar Apostolic, though it does not appear that he was ever officially informed of his appointment as Vicar Apostolic. Certainly the Chapter, who feared the nomination of someone who would prejudice or even destroy their style of government, were convinced that Howard was on their side in wanting the appointment of a canonical Bishop in

Ordinary. They were immovable in their demands. Apart from the question of confirming the Chapter's existence, the arguments were overwhelmingly in favour of a Vicar Apostolic with limited powers which could be gradually augmented until the English Church was ready for a formal hierarchy. In the event, because of the obstructiveness of the Chapter, but mainly because Charles II was forced to withdraw his support, the appointment of Howard foundered. The Chapter probably never knew that he had been appointed on the strict basis that he did not in word or deed recognize the authority of the Chapter.

In 1675 Howard left England on a routine visit to Bornhem. He was never to return. The Dominican friar, John Baptist Hackett, who had been such an influence on his early years was now the Pope's confessor and had used his position to advance his protégé. On Trinity Sunday 1675 a visitor arrived at Bornhem to announce to the astonished Howard and his tiny community that the Pope wished to confer on him the dignity of Cardinal. Among those who accompanied him from Bornhem to Rome where John Leyburn, the Secretary of the Chapter who had advocated Howard as Bishop and was to become his secretary and eventually the next Vicar Apostolic himself, and Howard's uncle William Stafford, executed in 1680 as a result of the Oates plot. On his arrival in Rome and elevation to the College of Cardinals, Howard was given the title of Santa Cecilia in Trastevere but in 1679 when it became vacant he was transferred to the great Dominican church of Santa Maria Sopra Minerva. He was placed on the staff of a number of Congregations, including those of Bishops and Regulars, the Council of Trent, Propaganda Fide, Sacred Rites and Relics.

As early as February 1676 the English Chapter were writing to Howard to remind him of the need for a Bishop, convinced that they now had a friend in high places. '... As for the other principle of a Bishop, When your Eminence sees it as seasonable to be moved for, our brethren humbly desire that no less authority be accepted than the Bishop of Chalcedon [Richard Smith] had, but if possible that it may be so absolutely ordinary that it may edify, not prejudice our body and so worded that bad friends may not trample upon it as they did upon his. This is all we conceive necessary to hint at present.'[5]

This was to be only the beginning of a long and tiresome correspondence between Howard and the Chapter over the question of a Vicar Apostolic or a Bishop. For the time being in England the whole matter had been dropped. The furore over the Declaration of Indulgence and the Oates Plot were making any changes in English Catholic circumstances unlikely. Howard himself was denounced by the plotters, allegedly being nominated as the new Archbishop of Canterbury in the event of a successful Catholic coup. Instead of which unlikely development, he found himself in March 1680 appointed Cardinal Protector of England and Scotland in succession to Cardinal Barberini who had died the previous year. Thus he was uniquely placed to influence affairs in England, but also to explain situations of great fragility to the Papacy and (it was hoped) moderate and guide the policies of Charles II and his headstrong brother. He was well aware of the problems and the disunity among Catholics in England, as he wrote in response to one letter of congratulation on his new post: 'If we were all united in hearts and minds as we are involved in the same persecution, what we suffer from the malice of our adversaries would be recompensed by the comfort received from one another, but the scandals arising from disagreements among ourselves ... do unfortunately deprive us of this advantage.'[6]

As Anstruther ruefully commented, 'The office of Cardinal Protector of England in those troublous times was no sinecure ...' He went on to describe the responsibilities involved. 'The Protector had very wide powers and control over all the English colleges on the Continent and was consulted at every turn by the various congregations on points touching the realms under his protection.

Now that the Protector was himself an Englishman and a member of Propaganda his influence was unusually strong. All the powers he had clamoured for while in England had now fallen into his lap, and with them a new caution and perhaps a sense of hopelessness that rendered them virtually ineffective.'[7]

The office of Cardinal Protector gave Howard authority over the English College in Rome, and no student could be admitted without his approval. How far he delegated that power to the Rector is unclear, but his name is always mentioned as the authority for each student's admission and later letters from the exiled Queen in the 1690s were sent directly to Howard on behalf of young men whom she commends to him as possible seminarians. One decree made by him in relation to the English College survives. Anstruther suggests that perhaps this was the only one necessary and the College was in good order. Another, less sanguine view, is that it was typical of others and is the only one to have survived in textual form. Either way, it suggests a close interest in day-to-day affairs. The decree of 13 December 1680 insists that morning meditation be made in common and that one of the priests be present to ensure that this is carried out. This insistence on common prayer (particularly if it was accompanied by other reforms) could well reflect Howard's enthusiasm for a particular style of clerical life.

Howard came into contact, possibly through the Royal Family, with Bartholomew Holzhauser, a Bavarian secular priest and mystic who met Charles II during the King's exile. He was only prevented with difficulty from embarking on the English mission himself despite total ignorance of the country and its language.[8] Holzhauser evolved a plan to foster a pattern of life for secular clergy by the formation of an 'Institute of Clerics Living in Common'. He was told by Rome that his ideal was so obvious as to need no official sanction, but under Innocent XI the Institute was canonically established by two Papal bulls of June 1680 and August 1684 – the first only weeks after

Howard's arrival in Rome. Howard saw the Institute as an admirable tool for restoring morale and unity among the English clergy. Its primary object was to have two or more priests living in common in the same house, without female attendance and in subjection (without the usual exemption for Regulars) to the Ordinary of the Diocese. In the Constitution of the Institute oddly no mention is made of the Divine Office as the form of common prayer, but emphasis is placed on the rosary, litanies, popular prayers and at least an hour of communal meditation (as insisted on by Howard at the English College). Anstruther, without indicating what the evidence was, mentions that, 'there is evidence that he contemplated imposing it on the English College in Rome, but nothing came of it.'[9] It seems that he introduced elements of it and certainly did his best to advocate it among the clergy already on the mission.

In 1684 Howard issued his only pastoral letter as Cardinal Protector to the English clergy and it is devoted wholly to the Institute. He expresses concern about the way of life of the English clergy, who were subject to three principle dangers: first that of idleness, second that of familiar everyday contact with women, third the uncontrolled administration of property, especially ecclesiastical property. He therefore commends the Institute to the secular clergy as the best solution.[10] It was not an overwhelming success, although it must be said that the ideal of a common life continued to re-emerge among the secular clergy and the Institute was used as a model by William Bernard Ullathorne in founding his diocesan seminary in the 1860s.

For Howard the lack of support for his introduction of the Institute was only part of the larger dispute over the organization and government of the English clergy. His advocacy of the Institute was a further irritant in the already tetchy relations with the Chapter of the English secular clergy. Howard's support and the opposition of the Chapter to a plan based on the assumed existence of a Bishop in Ordinary are telling. The Protector hoped to move towards Bishops in Ordinary in good time but a Bishop linked to the Institute was not in the Chapter's interests.

It was assumed by the Chapter that the Cardinal Protector was wholeheartedly in support of their aims and they were dismayed to find otherwise and that perhaps living in Rome had given him a different perspective. The question of Episcopal appointment does not reappear in correspondence until 1684 when it reveals a renewed lack of sympathy between Howard and the Chapter. In the summer of 1684 he issued his pastoral on the Institute and sent Thomas Codrington (his chaplain and secretary) and John Morgan to England to act as its advocates. They were both members of the Institute and had been appointed by the President of it to be procurators for the Institute in England. The Chapter were not impressed; a memorandum exists describing the Institute as, 'at present an impossibility and at best a future contingence whose very possibility is highly unlikely.'[11] It goes on to anticipate that the Institute would contribute to 'breaking the common bond of unity in the clergy by creating a separate body' and that it would be 'inconsistent with the common interest of the Chapter.' The general tone of the memorandum is that the Institute would create disunity, undermine the Chapter and add to disharmony rather than alleviate it. What underlay these comments was the belief that it would be a rival body which would reduce the influence of the Chapter.

In November of the same year, as if to reinforce the Chapter's self-conscious defence of its rights, formal letters were sent to Howard on the issue of Episcopal government. Acting, as they believed, canonically in *sede vacante*, they addressed Howard, expecting his agreement, on the need for a Bishop in Ordinary. After listing their nominees, the Chapter requested that, 'nothing be done inconsistent with the *esse* and *bene esse* of our Chapter.' Howard's reply discomfited the Chapter, as he bluntly regarded their insistence on a Bishop in Ordinary as having, 'more of nicety than substance in it.' In effect he argued the Roman view that, while the jurisdiction of a Vicar Apostolic would be ordinary in effect, it was not yet appropriate, 'without incurring greater inconveniences and dangers' to appoint a Bishop in Ordinary. The Chapter should be content with the authority vested in a Vicar Apostolic. However the real blow came when he addressed their comments on the standing of the Chapter and spelt out the reality that it continued to have no formal canonical standing. 'I have had, concerning this particular, several discourses with persons whose influence is strong upon deliberations of this kind and from them I find reason to conclude that your Chapter, upon the grounds it hath hitherto stood and doth at present stand, will not be allowed. It is here looked upon as illegal in its erection for want of authority in the erector and no less illegal in its continuation. Of this substantial defect they remain so persuaded that nothing allegeable in your behalf can be capable to remove the persuasion. It is not a Chapter they except against, but a Chapter standing upon such grounds as yours doth stand.'[12]

The Chapter, not surprisingly, were furious, not only at the dismissal of the issue of ordinary jurisdiction as a nicety, but even more at Howard's candid statement of the position of the Chapter in the official view of Rome. They hoped lamely that his personal view might be different and launched a fruitless history and defence of the Chapter.[13] James II shared the Chapter's distaste for the choice of a Vicar Apostolic and when John Leyburn was appointed in September 1685 he was displeased (despite the fact that both the King and Chapter favoured Leyburn personally). Leyburn had been secretary of the Chapter, yet now had to swear an oath not to recognize it. He and the three additional Vicars Apostolic gradually superseded the administrative role of the Chapter, which became little more than a gentlemanly clerical club.

Howard had played a major part in breaking the power of the Chapter. He was the prime mover in securing a rapid appointment as Vicar Apostolic when the opportunity presented itself. His secretary Leyburn, whose selection he doubtless guided, had wrested power in the Chapter from John Sergeant. He was the leader of the, 'long, skilful but increasingly desperate rear guard action against the inevitable: a defence of the vanishing secular clergy vision and of the historic and constitutional claims of the Chapter.'[14] It is no coincidence that Sergeant was the leading opponent of the Secular Clergy Institute, since, as Bossy says, 'Under his leadership the Chapter became a machine less for demanding ordinaries from Rome ... than for obstructing any efforts to introduce a different kind of regime.'[15] Howard's rise to power spelt the end for the Chapter and Sergeant's vision of English clerical organization, rendering his opponent in Bossy's view 'an anachronism'. Despite this, Sergeant continued to oppose all diminution of the Chapter's role. As late as 1697, after Howard's death, Sergeant wrote a passionate tract against the publication of the *Constitutions of the Secular Clergy Institute*, based on the memorandum drafted in 1684. At the heart of it was the now familiar argument that the Institute would undermine the Chapter and had 'sowed the seeds of perpetual dissension between the separating party and the standing body.'[16] Howard's advocacy of the Institute may have reached even beyond the grave. Perhaps out of piety for the memory of Howard who had sheltered his sons in Rome and seen one professed as a Dominican, the aged poet John Dryden wrote to the Secretary of State in 1697 in defence of the publisher of the *Constitutions*. As a result no action was taken against the publisher, who was also Sergeant's publisher and may even have been informed on by him.

Dryden's sons were not the only refugees in Rome to be grateful to Howard. As Cardinal Protector of the College of Convertiti (founded in 1540 for the instruction of convert Jews and Muslims) he opened its doors to converts from Protestantism. Pilgrims who had outstayed their welcome at the English College were often housed there. Others who received kindness were Lady Theophila Lucy, whom he received into the Church in 1681, Charles Wigmore and William Rixon both Worcestershire gentlemen who fled for their lives in 1679 under the shadow of the Oates plot, and Gilbert Burnet, later Bishop of Salisbury. He recorded, '... as he sheweth all the generous care and concern for his countrymen that they can expect from him, in so many obliging marks of his goodness for myself, as went far beyond a common civility, that I cannot enough acknowledge it.'[17] Anstruther remarked, with a sardonic edge, 'If the office of Cardinal Protector had involved no more than the relief of needy English Catholic exiles, then Howard was fully adequate for the task.'[18] There were others who thought him more useful.

The accession of the Catholic King James II was to greatly alter Howard's role in Rome. After the three days of feasting and celebrations hosted by Howard to mark the accession in March 1685, he moved his official residence into the new palace adjoining the English College. Here he furnished the staterooms, which he had designed and had built, with rich hangings given to him by Cardinals Altieri and Barberini. 'In May a crowd of students, doubtless of the English College, with drums and tambourines and other musical instruments and supported by a number of prelates, affixed the arms of England over the main door of Howard's new home.'[19] As the arms still quartered those of France it caused a minor diplomatic incident! There was to have been a solemn High Mass and *Te Deum* in the English College chapel on 27 May, with Madama Martinozzi, the Queen's aged grandmother as principal guest. Anstruther records inimitably what happened next. 'Alas, a few days before, she went to visit Howard's Flemish Ursulines and, convent floors being what they are, she fell from the top of the stairs to the bottom and was in no mood for a *Te Deum*. The celebration was postponed till the following Sunday and was attended by Howard and some thirty other prelates; the old lady rallied sufficiently to grace the occasion and then took to her bed and died.'[20]

As already noted, the new King pressed quickly for the appointment of Bishops and was annoyed to get only one and a Vicar Apostolic at that. It was rumoured that Howard was to go with Leyburn as extraordinary papal Nuncio, but in the end Archbishop Fernando d'Adda was sent. It was not long before Howard began to fear for the future of Catholic England under the reckless James and his advisers. His advice was for 'slow, calm and moderate courses', but, 'he saw that violent courses were more acceptable and would probably be followed.'[21] Despite his long standing service to the Stuarts, which continued until his death, Howard now entered a phase of misunderstanding and rough treatment by his royal patrons. It was not long before James II placed Howard in a delicate position by insisting on the appointment of a royal ambassador to Rome. His choice according to Anstruther was 'not felicitous'. Lord Castlemaine was chiefly known for being the husband of Charles II's favourite mistress and was described by the French Ambassador in London as 'rather ridiculous'.[22] D'Adda was received, at the King's insistence, as an official papal nuncio although he had not been sent as such. He therefore expected the same dignity to be granted to Castlemaine, which caused considerable embarrassment to the papal court and to Howard. Castlemaine's status was still not settled when he arrived at the gates of Rome and Howard was obliged to meet him and offer him hospitality at the English College. The situation and the individual clearly irritated the mild mannered Howard who tired of the College Rector whispering with the ambassador in late night clandestine meetings and threatened to break his neck over the College staircase. Within four days the ambassador was installed in a *palazzo* of the Doria-Pamphili in the Piazza Navona and the Rector was on his way home to England.

The main purpose of Castlemaine's embassy was not matters of Church and State, but the personal wishes of James and Mary of Modena, which was to embarrass the Cardinal Protector further and to severely strain his loyalty. Mary was anxious to see her uncle Rinaldo D'Este made a Cardinal and all the time she was Duchess of York Howard had pressed D'Este's cause whenever possible. The pressure, including direct letters from London to the Pope increased after the accession. No reply or explanation was ever forthcoming, out of delicacy. The fact was that the Prince Rinaldo was the heir presumptive of the childless Duke of Modena. Thus it would be unbecoming if the Duke died childless, for the Cardinal to resign in order to marry and perpetuate the line. Castlemaine raised the matter at only his second papal audience on 3 May and conveyed the delicate papal feelings to James. A report of 25 May, which Anstruther quotes without source, says, 'The English Ambassador, too impatient to await the return of his secretary with the reply from London from his King, and finding himself short of money, has decided to leave at once. To colour his departure with a more decorous pretext, he tells everybody that he has taken this resolution because he cannot stay here without loss of face as long as the Pontiff refuses the graces he asks for, and in particular the cardinalate for Prince Rinaldo.'[23] There was more to it than that. Finding that diplomacy had failed, he resorted to bullying and hectoring the Pope and threatened to leave Rome if his requests were not granted. The Pope responded by courteously reminding him that May was a cooler month for travel than June!

Eventually in August Howard persuaded the Pope to give way on D'Este. Despite his consistent loyalty to the Stuarts, Howard's policy of 'slow, calm and moderate courses' did not accord with that of the King. Where Howard was content to see Vicars Apostolic appointed until the time was right for Bishops in Ordinary, James wanted Bishops at once and more than one. Where Howard counselled the private and discreet exchange of royal and papal representation, James wanted the full panoply of ambassadorial pomp and ceremony. By the end of 1687 the King had lost confidence in Howard and had largely entrusted his affairs to D'Este – a cruel irony.

James pressed the Pope to make D'Este 'co-Protector' and used him in all-important matters. Howard continued to be useful in small exchanges but he was no longer the trusted intermediary. However, as his appointment was a papal one he remained Cardinal Protector till his death. He also retained his devotion to the King and Queen, after as well as before 1688. Gradually, trustful relations were re-established between the Cardinal and the exiled Court when Howard's influence was needed. The new Pope elected in October 1689 (Alexander VIII) refused to deal with D'Este and over the winter of 1690–91 relations between the Stuarts and Howard returned to something like the old days of trust and confidence. Nevertheless, even in his letter of condolence to the Pope on Howard's death, James could not resist pressing for D'Este as his successor. Howard's loyalty had never wavered. D'Este did precisely what was feared, succeeded as Duke of Modena and resigned his red hat in order to marry.

Howard died in his palace adjoining the English College in the early hours of 17 June 1694. Following the lying in state he was buried in his titular church of Santa Maria Sopra Minerva.[24] The bulk of Howard's estate went to the Dominican Order and the will resulted in an acrimonious lawsuit between the English College and the Order. It was claimed that the 10,000 *scudi* spent by Howard on the English College site was a loan not a gift. The counterclaim made by the College was for the loss of income incurred from the demolition of shops to make way for the new buildings. No clear outcome to the case has ever come to light. However it was acknowledged on both sides that Howard intended the new buildings to be incorporated into the College on his death. He built, as he planned, with an eye to a better future. His palace was scarcely built for personal ostentation, as he spent most of his time living as a friar at Santa Sabina. The palace was to give standing to the English College and to keep in the mind of Rome that the English Church was not merely a hole-in-the-corner remnant. As he spent the last months of his life destroying most of his papers, it is impossible to know what Howard's hopes were for the Stuarts and for a full restoration of Catholicism in England. His secretary Philip Ellis, O.S.B., as loyal himself to the Stuarts, in writing to inform James of Cardinal Howard's death was in no doubt that he had died of a broken heart and that the Stuarts bore some of the blame. 'I do not question but he will be more assisting to your Majesty where he is, and that his prayers will put an end to these sufferings of his King and country which his heart could no longer bear, but broke, to make way for the soul to take its flight towards heaven and be your agent there. It is certain grief was the principle cause of his death and he had no other cause for it besides that which relates to your Majesty.'[25]

Notes

1. C. R. Palmer, O.P., *Life of Philip Howard OP*, 1867.
2. Archives of the English Province of the Order of Preachers (Arch. OP), Anstruther Papers, Anstruther–Bullough, 1 April 1955.
3. Anstruther MS, Life of Philip Howard (Arch. OP) Chapter 5, pp. 110–11 [Chapter references are given as the pagination of the MS is unclear] Hereafter Anstruther MS.
4. J. Bossy, *The English Catholic Community 1570–1850*, 1975, p. 67.
5. Westminster Archdiocesan Archives (WAA) vol. 39 no. 103, Chapter–Howard, 25 February 1676.
6. Anstruther MS, Chapter 7, p. 4.
7. Anstruther MS, Chapter 7, p. 13. The tone of Anstruther's assessment of Howard is generally lukewarm bearing the implication that he was not really up to the job.
8. T. Birrell, *Holzhauser and England: Three Episodes, Grenzegange Literatur und Kultur im Kontext*, Amsterdam, 1990, pp. 453–63.
9. Anstruther MS, Chapter 7, p. 22.
10. WAA, vol. 39 no. 215, Howard to the Clergy of England and Scotland (printed).

11. WAA, vol. 39 no. 225, Observations by the Chapter by the Rule of the Institute (1684).
12. WAA, vol. 39 no. 231, Howard–Perrot, 19 January 1685.
13. WAA, vol. 39 no. 255, Draft letter, Chapter–Howard.
14. Bossy, op. cit., p. 67.
15. Ibid., p. 678.
16. J. Kirk, *Biographies of English Catholics*, 1909, pp. 50–51.
17. G. Burnet, *Some Letters Containing an account of what seemed most Remarkable in Switzerland, Italy etc.*, Amsterdam, 1686, Letter 4, 231.
18. Anstruther MS, Chapter 7, p. 50.
19. Anstruther MS, Chapter 8, p. 3.
20. Anstruther MS, Chapter 8, p. 4.
21. G. Burnet quoted in Anstruther MS, Chapter 8, p. 17.
22. Anstruther MS, Chapter 8, p. 13.
23. Anstruther MS, Chapter 8, pp. 33–4.
24. The tomb is not easily visible, being one of a group of stones set in the door behind the high altar.
25. Anstruther MS, Chapter 8, pp. 67–8.

This article originally appeared in the 1995 edition of 'The Venerabile' to commemorate the 300th Anniversary of Cardinal Howard's death.

Henry Benedict Stuart, Cardinal Duke of York

'Not Accepted by Men but Chosen by the Will of God': The Cardinal Duke of York

Nicholas Schofield

Ask the average Catholic to give a list of famous Marian shrines and it is likely to include Lourdes, Fatima, Loreto and Walsingham. A *Romano* might add *Divin' Amore*. But very few, I think, would mention the miraculous shrine of Our Lady outside the old English College summer *villa* at Monte Porzio.

Set in 1796, as revolutionary clouds loom, it is a drama in two acts for which our main source is a letter from Robert Smelt, the English bishops' agent in Rome.[1] Act One: an image of Our Lady is put up on the exterior walls of the Monte Porzio house. It soon begins to attract the devotion of the locals. One devotee of the image sees Our Lady move her eyes. Word of this wonderful happening spreads round the sleepy *Castelli* town like wild fire, and before long 'a great number of knives and offensive weapons' are hung up around the image, presumably as votive offerings. The Rector of the English College, Stefano Felici,[2] 'much pleased with all this, prepared a fine canopy and other ornaments'. Curtains close on the first Act; all seems well.

Act Two: the main character of the drama, at least as far as this essay is concerned, makes a grand entrance – the Bishop of Frascati, in whose diocese Monte Porzio lies, Cardinal Henry Benedict Stuart, known to his supporters as 'King Henry IX'. He orders the local curate to take the miraculous image into the church of St Gregory, just down the street. However, Rector Felici is not keen to lose the wonder-working picture, and produces the College's bull of foundation to show that it is exempt from the jurisdiction of the Ordinary. However the bishop still orders the curate to obey his mandate, and reminds Felici that he is 'both Bishop and King'. In the end, Felici wins after forbidding the curate to come near the villa and threatening that, should the picture be removed to the church, 'he would carry the boys in a body to the church, and take it away by force'. As an epilogue, Smelt adds that 'King Henry IX, who is as despotic a monarch as his ancestor Henry VIII, and full of logical contradiction, was violently enraged at the Rector and now abuses him like a pickpocket'. The shrine can still be seen, next door to what is now the *carabinieri* station.[3]

Brother of 'Bonnie Prince Charlie' and great-grandson of the unfortunate Charles I, failed military commander in the 'Forty-Five' and Dean of the College of Cardinals, Bishop of Frascati and King of Great Britain, the Cardinal Duke of York is a surprisingly neglected figure who deserves a re-examination.

Early Years

Henry Benedict Stuart was born on 6 March 1725 to 'James III', the 'Old Pretender', and Clementina Sobieski, granddaughter of John Sobieski, King of Poland, at the Palazzo Muti, sometimes called the *Palazzo dei Pretendenti*, near the Basilica of *Dodici Apostoli*. Christened by Benedict XIII himself, Prince Henry was proclaimed Duke of York – not a good omen since of the previous two, one had lost his head and the other his throne. As a child, he was noted for his handsomeness and charm, though he lacked his brother Charles' courage and adventurousness. He was also very pious. During the campaigns of 1745 the Marquis d'Argenson wrote that he 'never passes before a crucifix or an altar without genuflecting like a sacristan', whilst the Duc de Richelieu is reported to have told Henry: 'Your Royal Highness may perhaps win the Kingdom of Heaven by your prayers but never the kingdom of Great Britain'.

This is not surprising given the religiosity of his parents. His mother, encouraged by her Franciscan confessor, St Leonard of Port Maurice, spent her last years establishing needlework guilds that supplied needy churches with vestments and altar linen, and relieving destitute families. After her death in 1735, there was even talk of beatification – as late as 1771 Baron Ferdinand Sturm, 'noble of Hirschfeld and a Doctor of Medicine', attested to the curing of his son's 'putrid fever' through her intercession.[4] Her funeral served as one of the most poignant displays of honour to the exiled Stuarts. After lying in state for three days at *Dodici Apostoli*, surrounded by twenty-four wax candles and papal guards with drawn swords, she was taken to be buried at St Peter's in luscious robes and royal insignia, being followed by her household, various confraternities, as well as students of the *Venerabile* and the Irish and Scots Colleges. His father 'James III', also demonstrated a remarkable piety, sometimes verging on Jansenism, and after Clementina's death he spent hours in prayer before her monument at *Dodici Apostoli*.

Jacobitism and 'The Forty-Five'

The pseudo-court at Palazzo Muti was the centre of the Jacobite world by the time of Henry Stuart's birth. Given to the Stuarts by Clement XI in 1717, its entrance was guarded by papal cuirassiers, as at the Pope's own residences. In Rome 'James III' was treated with every mark of royal sovereignty. That is not to say that relations between the Vatican and the Stuarts were always easy. Clement's offer of a Roman *palazzo*, a *villa* at Albano and a decent pension had been somewhat half-hearted. The Papacy realized that excessive support for the unlucky dynasty could lead to retaliation both in the renewed attack on underground Catholics in England and possible aggression by the British naval arm in a vulnerable papal port such as Civitavecchia. Likewise, the Stuarts were well aware that their move to Rome was not good for 'PR' since their enemies delighted to associate the cause with the Scarlet Whore of Rome and to claim that the *dévot* 'Old Pretender' was 'priest-ridden' as he languished in the dark corners of his sombre palace. Such propaganda conveniently forgot that the Palazzo Muti was the unlikely location of an early experiment in ecumenism: the exiled Stuarts actually had papal dispensation to provide private Anglican services at their court for their many Protestant supporters.[5]

Jacobite contacts spread out north-westwards from this gloomy palace like a complex spider's web. Between Rome and London there were many pockets of exiles, forming a pan-European Jacobite Diaspora. Though cut off from their homeland and roots, many of these exiles fitted into continental society with relative ease, especially since *settecento* social elites shared a common, predominantly French culture. Moreover, in many towns, particularly in Flanders and northern France, there were pre-existing communities of British exiles, mostly Catholic. Of particular importance was the string of religious houses and seminaries. James II himself had been buried at St Edmund's, the English Benedictine Priory in Paris,[6] which quickly became a Jacobite mausoleum – and many of these exiled religious were staunch supporters of the 'Good Old Cause'. For example, Thomas Southcott, President of the English Benedictine Congregation

(1721–41), was involved in hatching plots, gathering information for the Pretenders and attempting to influence diplomacy at the highest levels.[7] Many of the Jacobite exiles proved useful additions to their host nations: Thomas Gordon is seen as one of the founders of the Russian Navy, John Holker built up the French textiles industry and Maximilian Ulysses Browne successfully campaigned for Austria against Frederick the Great and was made a count.[8]

The first half of the eighteenth century saw repeated Jacobite attempts to regain the British throne, often in alliance with other rulers who had an eye on Europe's ever-shifting balance of power. Jacobitism was a vague and fluid movement, linked to a variety of conservative causes such as the Divine Right of Kings, Catholicism and Scottish interest in a Stuart restoration, as well as the age-old factor of personal interest. Motives for supporting the Stuarts were tremendously variable. Protestants and Catholics fought for the cause side by side in the rebellions of 1715 and 1745, and perhaps as many as eight of London's Lord Mayors in the 1740s had strong Jacobite sympathies. Even Dr Johnson could be numbered amongst its adherents, although he told Boswell on the reception of his royal pension that he thought 'the pleasure of cursing the House of Hanover and drinking King James' health are amply overbalanced by £300 a year'.[9] As a military force, Jacobitism was largely dependent on the support of the Highland clans, English (often 'Tory') enthusiasts and French aid in the form of money, arms and personnel. Indeed, fear of a Franco-Jacobite invasion of England was a constant during these years: in 1739 Walpole was unwilling to send a strong fleet to the West Indies during a war with Spain for this very reason. Whatever the chances of a successful Jacobite rising may have been, the threat dominated the political imagination in the same way as the Elizabethans had feared a Spanish invasion backed by recusant gentry, 'Fifth Columnist' Jesuits and the Vatican. Perhaps the British government was right to be afraid. The

'Glorious Revolution' of 1688 had shown what a potent force a rebellion could be when supported by a small invasion force. The happenings inside the Palazzo Muti were thus of international import and not just a curiosity concerning royal might-have-beens.

The last great Jacobite push, the celebrated 'Forty-Five', coincided with Henry's youth and marked a turning point in his life and Stuart fortunes. It originated with Louis XV's invitation to Charles to discuss an invasion at the end of 1743. With the fall of Walpole, the emergence of a sympathetic French Chief-Minister, the Cardinal de Tencin (who reputedly owed his red hat to James' influence at the Vatican), and English involvement in the War of the Austrian Succession, it seemed like a propitious opportunity. Charles left for Paris in complete secrecy during a shooting expedition at Cisterna with his brother, who only found out what had happened several days later. An initial attempt to open hostilities was foiled by the weather, which had driven back the Jacobite fleet, Charles and the talented Comte de Saxe narrowly escaping death. There followed a considerable period during which Charles waited at Gravelines, convinced of the loss of French interest and that he should perhaps act alone.

The moment came in the summer of 1745 – Saxe had defeated the British at Fontenoy, George II was in Hanover and his army in Flanders was in disarray, while the domestic military presence was weak. Charles set off from Belle-Ille for Scotland on 5 July 1745. Thanks to the military genius of Lord George Murray, there were early successes – the entry into Edinburgh, the victory at Prestonpans, the invasion of England, which got as far south as Derby – which reawakened the French from their slumbers. Prince Henry represented Stuart interests at a meeting with Louis XV at Fontainbleau in the October of that year and was given nominal command of a French-supported invasion force of 10,000 that assembled at Dunkirk, though the Duc de Richelieu was in real control. However, the expedition was delayed and finally called-off after Charles' defeat – indeed, for many years Jacobites accused Richelieu of being a Hanoverian puppet, eager to put off action. It became clear at this juncture that Henry was not a second 'Bonnie Prince' for he lacked his brother's military ardour and political talent, and preferred religion – Richelieu, as we have already noted, saw him as an 'Italian bigot'. Over the Channel the hopes engendered by Charles' early triumphs were soon ended – without French aid, he withdrew from Derby, and it was back in the Highlands at Culloden that his great adventure was crushed in little over forty minutes.

Cardinal

Charles saw Culloden as a temporary setback and began thinking of plans of recovery. Meanwhile Henry thought it time to announce a step he had long been meditating – entrance to the clerical state. He was tonsured by Benedict XIV on 30 June 1747 and received the red hat on 3 July. This move has often been seen as a 'second Culloden' to the Stuart cause, and resulted in an eighteen-year separation from his furious brother. Having the second-in-line to the throne as a Roman Cardinal was anything but a plus for the Jacobites, who hoped to regain a Protestant crown, and Charles' feelings on the matter may partly explain his temporary conversion to Anglicanism during a trip to London in 1750 in the hope of increasing support. However, though it is dangerous to dabble in the realm of historical 'if's', it is unlikely that a Jacobite King would have been plausible after the disaster of 1745, and one can perhaps see Henry's move from throne to altar as the result of personal discernment and political realism. Moreover, it is possible that, initially, the idea was for Henry, like many other Cardinals, to remain in Minor Orders and use the office to collect substantial revenues, so that he could be released from the clerical status should he be called to head the family. However, on 1 September 1748 Henry was ordained a priest and became a Cardinal Priest a few days later.

Thus the Duke of York received the red hat at the age of twenty-two. He was not the first English prince to assume the sacred purple, for Henry Beaufort, the son of John of Gaunt, and Reginald Pole, Edward IV's great-nephew, had gone before him. In consideration of York's high rank, he was given various special privileges. For example, he could sit in the pope's presence on a chair with an embroidered cushion rather than a wooden stool, and wore the royal ermine on his *mozetta*. He was also given precedence after the Dean of the College of Cardinals. These privileges were taken seriously by Henry, though they greatly annoyed many of the other cardinals, and led to various disputes over matters of ecclesiastical etiquette which might seem trivial to us but were important in an age of hierarchy and order.

Cardinal York was given the titular church of Santa Maria in Campitelli, famous for the wonder-working *Madonna del Portico*. In 1751 James III granted a sum of money to the church for the purpose of promoting a society that met there weekly to pray for the conversion of Great Britain, and it seems that both James and Henry regularly attended these services, together, no doubt, with students from the English-speaking colleges in Rome. This service continued into the twentieth century.[10] This spiritual concern for England is also revealed in Benedict XIV's extension in January 1749 of the feasts of SS George, Augustine, Edward, Ursula, Edmund and Thomas to 'all ecclesiastics of the English nation wheresoever living' at the instigation of the new Cardinal. These feasts had previously only been granted to the English College and the English Province of Jesuits.[11]

In the great epic of the English College's history, Cardinal York makes only fleeting appearances. We know that he was present at the Requiem Mass offered for 'the Old Pretender' at the College on 24 January 1766, and in 1791 he congratulated the *Venerabile* after the repeal of the

Penal Laws. The Cardinal-King also seems to have supported the 1792–4 campaign to obtain English seculars for the College staff.[12] Otherwise we can only speculate about his relationship with the *Venerabile*. As one of the longest-ever serving cardinals (1747–1807) and an inhabitant of the nearby *Cancelleria*, he would have been a familiar figure to the students. The College, however, had to be careful about its Jacobite links. On 31 March 1766 'Bonnie Prince Charlie' had visited the College, heard Mass in the Tribune and allowed students to kiss his hand, but the rumour then spread that he had been crowned in the church as 'Charles III' and consequently the Rector, Charles Booth, was expelled.[13]

Given his position, it is little surprise that York quickly became loaded with honours and titles. He was made Archpriest of St Peter's (1749),[14] Vice-Chancellor (1763), an office which gave him the residence of the *Cancelleria*, and eventually Dean of the College of Cardinals (1803). His biographers often name him as *Camerlengo* of the Holy Roman Church, an official who organized Conclaves and had considerable powers during the *Sede Vacante*, coining money and issuing edicts. However, as Michael Sharp has shown, this is highly unlikely, though he was appointed *Camerlengo* of the Sacred College of Cardinals in 1758 and 1759, an appointment given only for a year.[15] From Louis XV he received the rich Abbeys of Auchin (1748) and St Amand (1752), and he also possessed prebends and benefices in Spain and Mexico. In 1767 Sir William Hamilton estimates his income from his Roman and French benefices to have been around £18,000 a year,[16] and his Spanish benefices and private fortune must have put that figure up to at least £30,000.

Eighteenth-century cardinals were wealthy, cultured and often worldly. Cardinal Ottoboni, for example, wrote an opera entitled *Colombo*, and supposedly had his bedroom painted with the portraits of his various mistresses disguised as virgin saints. York was highly refined and became an important figure on the Roman social circuit. He relished the society of musicians, commissioning pieces such as Porpora's *Magnificat a 8*, and entered into a feud with his father after he privately entertained the choir master at Santa Maria in Campitelli, the son of a mere barber. Here, Henry took after his grandfather, James II, who even in exile at Saint-Germain employed the likes of François Couperin.[17] However, despite his evident hospitality he seems to have had a reputation of being a bore – Benedict XIV once exclaimed that 'if all the Stuarts were as boring as he, no wonder the English drove them out'.

Doubts have often been raised over the Cardinal's sexuality. In 1794, Mrs Piozzi reported rumours that York kept 'a catamite publicly at Rome', and Benedict XIV thought that he was a good priest in need of a guiding hand, even hoping in a letter of January 1756 that he would not use money from a recently acquired French abbey *'en choses criminelles'*.[18] Count Goranni reported that his palace was 'filled with young adolescents of beautiful aspect, but in clerical dress'. His 'favourites' included Father Lercari, his *maestro di camera*, to whom, as Horace Walpole commented, the young Cardinal 'entirely abandoned himself', and the future Cardinal Ercole Consalvi, an orphan educated at Frascati seminary and treated like a son in York's household. But we should not read too much into such reports for equally clear in contemporary sources is York's proper and virtuous nature and horror of all impropriety. His biographer, Mastrofini, called him in the exaggerated language of the time 'spotless as the morning snow, virgin as the lily-of-the-valley'.[19]

Bishop of Frascati

In 1758 the newly-elected Clement XIII nominated York Archbishop of Corinth *in partibus infidelium*, and the following year he renounced his 'title' of Santa Maria in Campitelli, taking up in its place Santa Maria in Trastevere (where one can still see his coat of arms on the right of the High Altar). On 13 July 1761 York was nominated as Bishop of Frascati, one of the six 'suburbican' sees of Rome. Six days later he solemnly took possession of the See, his father, as 'King of England', occupying a throne on the right of the sanctuary, and the locals celebrated with bonfires and illuminations. The fountain in the Piazza Maggiore was made to flow red wine. He took up residence at the episcopal palace, *La Rocca*, which was in such bad repair that at a banquet in September 1775 the floor gave way throwing the guests into the coach house below, killing one of the guests, though the Cardinal fortunately landed safely on a coach roof. Not surprisingly, the Cardinal Bishop decided to make several alterations.

One biographer has spoken of his days at Frascati as spent 'in pious meditation, in vast and varied charity, and in princely entertainment'.[20] There is much truth in this somewhat simplistic and idyllic statement. As one of the richest Italian Cardinals, he could afford to keep a sumptuous court. His stables contained sixty horses, ready for the regular trips in and out of Rome, and the Cardinal's love of speed became legendary during his own day. For example, on the way to a reception held by Cardinal de Bernis to celebrate the birth of Louis XVI's heir one of York's lackeys, known as 'Gigi', thrust a burning torch into the faces of Princess Rezzonico's steeds in order to prevent her carriage from arriving first.[21] At the same time, we find something of the contemplative in him, as seen in the long hours he spent in his library, perhaps reading St Augustine, his favourite theologian.

Most remarkable was the Cardinal's considerable pastoral ability and zeal. He took his responsibilities as a bishop seriously. As a consequence Cardinal Wiseman could write that 'the diocese of Frascati was full, when I first knew it, of recollections of the Cardinal Duke, all demonstrative of his singular goodness and simplicity of character',[22] and by the time of his death he was known as 'Protector of the Poor'. He founded schools and orphanages, and was generous in giving alms. This extended beyond the confines of Frascati: a chemist shop opposite the *Cancelleria* in Rome had an arrangement whereby the poor could obtain whatever medicines they needed at his expense. He called diocesan synods in 1763 and 1776 which not only dealt with clerical discipline and theological and sacramental questions but issues such as blasphemy, swearing, alcoholism, violence to women and rape. He published a pamphlet on *Sins of the Drunkard*.[23] He also rebuilt the diocesan seminary that had been founded by Cardinal Cesi in the mid-sixteenth century, founded bursaries for poor students, and established a fine library there, the *Biblioteca Eboracense*. This seminary, like the Cathedral, was severely damaged in the bombing of 1943–4. Less happy was his building of a Passionist monastery on Monte Cavo in 1788, requiring the demolition of the important Roman temple of Jupiter Latialis, thus making York guilty of one of the great acts of eighteenth century 'ecclesiastical vandalism' and open to the abuse of modern classicists and art-lovers.

The Cardinal King

'Bonnie Prince Charlie' died in 1788 at the age of sixty-eight. His life after Culloden had been disastrous. Banished from France in 1748, he had plunged into the depths of alcoholism after the failure of the 'Elibank Conspiracy', a plot to capture the Royal Family in 1751. Two years later a daughter, Charlotte, was born to his mistress, Clementina Walkinshaw. Legitimized as the Duchess of Albany in 1784, she went on to bear three daughters as mistress to the Prince Archbishop of Bordeaux. In 1772 Charles married Louise of Stolberg, but she took lovers, retired to a convent with half of his annual pension, and after his death had relationships with the poet, Count Vittorio Alfieri and the painter, François Xavier Fabre.

The Cardinal arranged a Solemn Requiem for his brother at Frascati Cathedral, where he was laid to rest until he was transferred to St Peter's in 1807. The Cardinal, who remained a great stickler for royal titles and prerogatives, decided to strike medals to celebrate his succession with the inscription: *Hen IX. Mag. Brit. Fr. et Hib. Rex. Fid. Def. Card. Ep. Tusc.* On the reverse was an allegory of Religion, with a lion at her feet, holding a large cross and looking sadly at a crown and a red hat lying on the ground, and the words *Non Desideriis Hominum sed Voluntate Dei* (Not accepted by men but chosen by the will of God). A crown replaced the coronet on his coat of arms and his Household was instructed to call him 'Majesty'. In official documents he was referred to as *Dux Eboracensis nuncupatus* – 'called Duke of York', for he was now truly King. A Scots visitor of 1802–3, Joseph Forsyth, tells us that the Cardinal paid no visits except to the Pope and the ex-King of Sardinia, and that during meals guests did not break the silence until Henry IX had first spoken, both vestiges of royal ceremony.[24]

Most strikingly, he continued the ancient custom of touching (with medals) sufferers of the 'King's Evil', scrofula. This was the disease that had afflicted Samuel Johnson during his youth, blinding him temporarily in one eye. He had been taken to London to be 'touched' by Queen Anne, who he remembered as 'a lady in diamonds and a long black hood'. However he was not cured. Boswell 'ventured to say to him, in allusion to the political principles in which he was educated, and of which he retained some odour [i.e. Jacobitism], that his mother had not carried him far enough; she should have taken him to Rome'[25] – presumably to be touched by the pretender royals. The story even abounded that the Cardinal touched the Duke of Gloucester, George III's delinquent brother, present at one of the ceremonies, though he pretended not to notice. Indeed, the College Pilgrim Books for the period contain the names of those who travelled to Rome for these ceremonies.[26] As late as 1901 a handkerchief stained with the Cardinal King's blood kept in Ireland was thought to cure the 'King's Evil'.[27] The Cardinal King became the last English 'monarch' to subscribe to this rite, which implied a deep belief in the Divine Right of Kings, although it lingered on in France until the reign of Charles X.

The succession of Henry IX, though expressed in the unmistakable language of *de jure* Kingship, was treated as a subject of pleasantry and curiosity by the few of his subjects who heard of it. This showed how much things had changed since the heady days of 1745 when the son of the Earl of Derwentwater, freshly captured off the Kentish coast, was nearly lynched by a London mob that believed this young Jacobite to be none other than the Duke of York himself. A combination of increasingly good relations between the Vatican and St James' following papal recognition of the House of Hanover on the death of the 'Old Pretender', and the realization that a celibate Roman Cardinal posed little threat to a well-established Protestant monarch such as George III meant that ambivalent attitudes towards the Stuart claimants were watered down. Henry IX was seen as little more than a charming relic of a noble house that had suffered countless misfortunes over the years.

Revolution

The year after the Cardinal's succession, the Bastille was stormed and France was plunged into revolution. In 1793 Louis XVI went to the scaffold just as Henry's great-grandfather had done in 1649. The Cardinal held a solemn Mass for the King's soul at Frascati. In 1794 he learnt that he had lost the important incomes from his French Abbeys, and in 1796 Napoleon invaded Italy. To aid the Pope, Henry disposed of the Stuart jewels, including the famous Sobieski ruby valued at £50,000, and was reduced to a state of some distress. Soon afterwards, General Berthier occupied Rome and a Republic was declared on 15 February

1798, the anniversary of the Pope's election. Pius VI was placed under 'protective custody'. The Cardinal King took refuge first at Naples, then, after brief stays in Messina and Corfu, went to Venice, where he took lodgings near the Rialto. Meanwhile, the forces of revolution even reached the little town of Frascati, led by a forward thinking Canon and Professor of Theology at the Seminary, who planted a 'Tree of Liberty' on the heights of Tusculum.

There is a tradition that Henry, now in desperate straits, was entangled in the Irish Rebellion of 1798. There is little evidence for his active involvement, although Napoleon, reviving the Bourbon policy of using Jacobite rhetoric to harass England, threatened to forcefully set the Cardinal on the throne through the backstairs of Ireland. However, rather like the earlier idea of setting Charles up as ruler of a newly independent America, this came to nothing. The period actually showed the strengthening of Henry's relations with Great Britain, partly because the various crises of the 1780s and 1790s drew traditional elites closer together whatever their previous differences had been. In 1794 a detachment of British troops was even stationed at Civitavecchia to aid the harassed Pope. An article in *The Times* of 28 February 1800 sums up this sympathetic opinion: quoting Voltaire's famous statement about the House of Stuart that 'there is no instance in history of any family being unfortunate for so great a length of time', it adds to his account of misfortunes the 'placid, humane, and temperate' Henry who, 'at a period of life when least able to struggle with misfortune', found himself 'driven from his Episcopal residence; his houses sacked; his property confiscated, and driven to seek his personal safety in flight upon the seas, under every aggravated circumstance that could affect his health and fortunes!'[28] With the help of the representations of Cardinal Borgia, a fellow exile in Venice, and Sir John Coxe-Hippisley, the Cardinal was granted a royal pension by George III of £5,000 annually as a proof of his affection and esteem. The Cardinal was deeply appreciative of this mark of royal favour from his rival, although he cannot have helped think of the £50,000 life annuity voted by Parliament to his grandmother, Mary of Modena, in 1685 which had never been paid.

The Twilight Years

Pius VI died a prisoner in the citadel of Valence on 29 August 1799, after a pontificate of twenty-four years. Many assumed the demise of the Holy See, but Pius had left instructions for the holding of a conclave in emergency conditions. The cardinals met at San Georgio in Venice under Austrian protection. Although as a senior cardinal Henry stood a reasonable chance of becoming England's first King-Pope, the Benedictine Cardinal Chiaramonte was elected as Pius VII after a fourteen-week stalemate. He re-entered Rome on 3 July 1800, being welcomed by Henry on the steps of St Peter's, and named Consalvi, a scion of Frascati seminary, as his Secretary of State.

The Cardinal King was thus able to take re-possession of his diocese, and returned to his old life, though limited by increasing frailty. We see in Cesarini's detailed diary that Henry continued to attend to his Episcopal duties, touch for the King's evil, receive guests at his open table, especially travellers from his Kingdom which he had never visited. At Easter 1807 he was especially pleased to receive Pitt's niece. One of the Cardinal's favourite companions during these last years was a stray dog that had attached itself to him at the gate of St Peter's – an occurrence which was interpreted as a recognition of his royal blood since the dog, being supposed a King Charles spaniel, was instinctively acquainted with the Stuarts.[29]

In 1803 Henry was made Dean of the College of Cardinals, and with it Bishop of Ostia and Velletri, but given his advanced age this was little more than an honorary title and made little difference to Henry's way of life. The office gave him the privilege of crowning the next Pope, though he never lived long enough to do this. With the permission of the Pope he was allowed to keep his Frascati residence, though no longer bishop there. During these last years York suffered from a mild form of epilepsy, causing long lapses of memory and putting control of his diocese into the hands of his Vicar-General. He was seen in 1804 entering St Peter's in procession 'with a far away look in his eyes'.

The end, however, was sudden. Taken ill on 10 July 1807, 'Henry IX' died peacefully at *La Rocca* on the fourth day of his illness, the forty-sixth anniversary of his translation to Frascati. The *de jure* Crown passed to his cousin, Charles Emmanuel IV of Savoy.

Taken to Rome the following day, Henry's body lay in state at the *Cancelleria* for three days, not so much as King but as an eminent Roman Cardinal, a venerable dinosaur from the *ancien regime*. The Requiem was sung at Sant' Andrea della Valle and the Cardinal buried in St Peter's, where his brother joined him from his temporary tomb at Frascati. At the instigation of Pius VII, Canova's magnificent classical monument was erected in memory of *Jacobo III*, *Karolo Eduardo* and *Henrico Decano Patrum Cardinalium*, financed partly by George IV. More recently, it was restored thanks to the generosity of Queen Elizabeth the Queen Mother.

So perished the House of Stuart. Voltaire marvelled at the tragedy of the dynasty, drawing up a long list of doom stretching from the assassinated James I (of Scotland) through two family encounters with the headsman on the scaffold to the failures of the exiled Jacobites. 'If anything', he added, 'could justify those who believe in an "unavoidable fatality", it would be the continued succession of misfortunes which have befallen the House of Stuart during the space of above three hundred years'. Surely the person of Henry Stuart, a dignified, devout, even courageous Cardinal full of pastoral zeal, though far from perfect, shed a ray of light as the sun set upon the tired Stuart day.

Notes

1. The main source for this incident is a letter dated 15 October 1796 from Fr Robert Smelt, agent of the English bishops in Rome, quoted in *The Venerabile*, vol. III, no. 3 (October 1927), 265–6.
2. Rector, 1787–98.
3. In 1905 Pius X granted an indulgence for the shrine on the Third Sunday in July and the Feast of the Immaculate Conception (see VEC Archives M433). It remains a spiritual focus in the town to this day.
4. H. M. Vaughan, *The Last of the Royal Stuarts* (1906), pp. 9–10, quoting British Library Add Ms. 34,638, f.247 (1781).
5. Interestingly Louis XIV refused to grant such permission during the Stuarts' sojourn at Saint-Germain. Religious nonconformity was illegal in France after the Revocation of the Edict of Nantes in 1685.
6. Revolutionaries removed the body for public exhibition in 1793, before its destruction in 1794. 'Relics' of James II were, however, amazingly widespread: the English Benedictine nuns of Dunkirk claimed a wax death mask; the English Augustinian nuns of Paris treasured some flesh taken from his right arm; his entrails were divided between Saint-Germain-en-Laye and the English Jesuits at Saint-Omer; the Scots College, Paris even kept his brain in a lead box. To this day, pieces of linen dipped in his blood can be found at Ushaw, Stonyhurst, Downside and Sizergh.
7. G. Scott, *Gothic Rage Undone: English Monks in the Age of the Enlightenment*, 1992, pp. 190–200.
8. D. Szechi, *The Jacobites: Britain and Europe 1688–1788*, 1994, pp. 126–30.
9. J. Boswell, *Life of Dr Samuel Johnson*, Penguin, 1979, pp. 108–9.
10. In 1898 Leo XIII ordered a solemn *triduum* of prayer at this church for the conversion of England – this was at the time of the debate on the validity of Anglican Orders. The Campitelli prayers seem to have been said until recently. See J. Cartmell, 'Santa Maria in Portico', in *The Venerabile*, vol. II, 1 (October 1924), 29–30 and VEC Archives. Scr.73.8.1.
11. H. Thurston in *The Month*, vol. CXI (March 1908), 280.
12. B. Tucker, 'The Cardinal King of England' in *The Venerabile*, vol. XVIII, 3 (November 1957, 135–49.

13. Ibid., 138. See also R. L. Stewart's '1766 and all that' in *The Venerabile*, vol. XV, 4 (May 1952), 266–70.
14. The Cardinal soon made his authority felt – one of his first official acts was to rebuke a Canon who had dared to sit in choir with his hair powdered.
15. M. Sharp, 'Henry, Cardinal (Camerlengo?), Duke of York' in *Royal Stuart Review*, vol. 7, 4 (1990), 57–60. The only coins struck by Cardinal York during a *Sede Vacante* were as Vice-Chancellor, not as *Camerlengo*, in 1769 and 1774. I am most grateful to Mr B. Tucker for bringing my attention to this.
16. The altar of the private oratory on the *piano nobile* was consecrated by Cardinal York and contains the inscription: *Henr. Epis. Tusc. S.R.E. Vicecan. Card. Dux. Eborac. Alt. Hoc. Consecr. Die. X. Nov. MDCCLXIV.*
17. Couperin composed a series of *petit motets* for James II.
18. Vaughan, op. cit., p. 65.
19. J. Lees-Milne, *The Last Stuarts*, 1983, pp. 151–4.
20. Vaughan, op. cit., p. 149.
21. Ibid., p. 71.
22. N. Wiseman, *Recollections of the Last Four Popes*, 1858, p. 102 (footnote).
23. A. Shield, *Henry Stuart, Cardinal of York and his Times*, 1908, p. 274 (footnote).
24. Vaughan, op. cit., pp. 257–8.
25. Boswell, op. cit., p. 39. Queen Anne was the last British monarch to touch for scrofula, using a simplified rite, though it remained in the official prayer book until 1732 (English editions) and 1759 (Latin editions).
26. VEC Archives, *Liber 292*. See also *Liber 1680* (The Estates of Cardinal York) which records the striking of scrofula medals (*Medaglione delle Scrofule*) by the *Incisore Camerale*, Giovanni Hamerani, in July and August 1801, May 1802 and October 1803.
27. M. Bloch, *The Royal Touch*, 1981, p. 223.
28. See *The Times*, 28 February 1800, quoted in P. Bindelli, *Enrico Stuart, Cardinale Duca di York*, 1982, pp. 256–7.
29. Shield, op. cit., p. 291 and Vaughan, op. cit, pp. 258–9.

This article first appeared in the 1999 edition of 'The Venerabile'.

Julian Watts-Russell in his Zouave uniform.

Julian Watts-Russell and the Papal Zouaves[1]

Richard Whinder

Standing just inside the door to the church of the English College, the visitor comes across the plain and rather battered monument to an almost forgotten Englishman. The words carved on the marble cylinder state the bare facts of the case:

> Julian Watts-Russell – Papal Zouave – died aged seventeen years and ten months – the youngest to fall at the battlefield of Mentana

As a monument it scarcely bears comparison with the baroque splendours of the Dereham memorial nearby, raised to commemorate the last scion of that ancient family, who preferred to embrace perpetual bachelorhood, rather than marry and risk raising heirs who might abandon the True Faith or the Jacobite cause. Nor does the epitaph compare with the one adjacent, composed to commemorate that pattern of perfection, Martha Swinburne, the nine-year old prodigy who was the last person to be laid to rest in the medieval church. Yet, there was a time when the name of Julian Watts-Russell seemed destined to shine among the ranks of the canonized saints – at least if one energetic English cleric had had his way.

We might well ask then, what was the story of this youthful martyr for Papal sovereignty, or the history of the strangely named band of troops for which he fought?

The context is that of the final years of the Papal States, when the Bishop of Rome still ruled as Pope and King over the City and its adjoining regions. The heart of this kingdom was of course Rome itself, the Patrimony of St Peter. To the north the Papal States included Umbria, and towards the Adriatic coast, the Marches, and Ancona. Finally, there was the Romagna, in the southern part of the plain of Po, which included the cities of Bologna and Ravenna. Confiscated by Napoleon I, but restored by the Congress of Vienna in 1815, this temporal power of the Pope was at once the papacy's burden and its guarantee of security. Menaced by the dread approaches of an atheistic modernity, the popes clung to this remnant of civil monarchy in the fear that, were the occupant of the Holy See to be the subject of any other political power, the papacy's freedom of action might be fatally compromised. The danger was especially great if, God forbid, the power in question was a disciple of the revolutionary principles of 1789. And so, in the face of liberal opinion, and, above all, in opposition to those who longed for a unified Italy governed by a single ruler, the popes did all they could to maintain intact their temporal authority, and to resist anything that seemed to challenge it. Pius VII (1800–1823) changed the flag of the Papal States – previously the red and gold colours used from antiquity and still used today by the *Comune di Roma* – and adopted the white and gold colours familiar today, apparently since revolutionary red had no place in the insignia of a pope. Gregory XVI (1831–1846) opposed any modernization whatsoever, declaring that the Papal States were lost forever if a single railway line were to be allowed to pass through them, and regarding with horror such innovations as gas lighting for the streets. Not that this good and intelligent man was a mere unthinking reactionary. In his governance of the Church, on the contrary, Gregory proved to be something of an innovator. He was the first author of a papal encyclical (*Mirari vos*, 1832), and a fervent patron of the missions (which he established in Abyssinia, India, China and Polynesia, among other places). He was far-sighted enough to pave the way for the restoration of a proper hierarchy in England and Wales (doubling the number of Vicars Apostolic to eight). Yet this willingness to embrace new methods was entirely absent from his way of government as a temporal monarch. Here, conservatism and timidity reigned. Any change, the pope feared, must inevitably undermine the time-honoured, theocratic character of the Papal States. Trains would bring sceptical, freethinking literature pouring in from the Godless countries of the north, and by uniting provinces long separated by geography, would weaken the particular identity of the Italian cities, and the influence which their bishops could wield over these tiny dioceses. Street lighting could only dim the vision of the trackless wastes of the night sky, the movement of the spheres that was such an eloquent illustration of the providence of God. Moreover, the garishness of gas lighting would detract from the votive candles of the faithful, flickering before the countless *Madonnelle* of Rome. And so Pope Gregory set his heart against change and declared that everything must always be as it always had been before. Outwardly, perhaps, it was so. As the Pope travelled in his golden coach, flanked by pontifical dragoons, through the towns and villages on his way to Frascati or Castelgandolfo, triumphal arches were still erected by a seemingly contented populace, and as he fished contentedly in the still waters of Lake Albano (a favourite pastime), Gregory perhaps imagined that this legacy of changelessness could outlast him. But it was not to be. Maintaining an essentially feudal state against the depredations of the modern world could not be done without the authoritarian use of force and fear. There was weariness too with a civil administration dominated by tonsured clerics, of economic stagnation and crying poverty. The happy crowds who waved to their Pontiff in his splendid coach were at the same time exasperated by censorship and repression, by the spies at every street corner and the informers and policemen who dogged one's every step. There was a desperate longing for change, and by the beginning of the reign of Giovanni Mastai-Ferretti – crowned as Pope Pius IX in 1846 – that longing had turned to a clamour. At first, it seemed that *Pio Nono* would be willing to respond.

The new Pope was humble, friendly, outgoing and open. In contrast to the austere and ascetic Gregory, Pius laughed and joked and consumed enormous quantities of snuff, which, to his courtiers' displeasure, he frequently spilt down the front of his white soutane. He left his palaces of the Quirinal and the Vatican to visit the ordinary people, celebrating Mass in convents and parish churches. He introduced gas lamps, and even built some railway lines, along which he travelled in his specially constructed pontifical coach. He granted an amnesty to political prisoners, a gesture which met with huge acclaim, and finally – a thing unthinkable to his conservative predecessors – he granted the Papal States a constitution. It seemed that the Papacy had at last thrown in its lot with the forces of progress, and *Pio Nono* was acclaimed as a popular hero. The impact on his contemporaries, in fact, can be meaningfully compared to that of Pope John XXIII a generation ago.[2] But just as Pope John's *aggiorniamento* was not welcomed by everyone with open arms, so too Pius IX's openness to change was regarded with horror by his more reactionary contemporaries. The archconservative Chancellor of Austria, the architect of post-Napoleonic Europe, Count Metternich, shuddered for the future, declaring that he had made provision for everything except a liberal pope. A discontented Cardinal was heard to comment that even the cats were liberals in the Mastai-Ferretti household. Then, just as Pope Pius was being feted as a model of progressive values, disaster struck.

1848 saw a wave of revolts all over Europe, as the long

repressed spirit of revolution broke free again. Metternich's system, as he had foreseen, was blown to pieces, and the principles of 1789 were resurgent once more. Monarchies fell, and those that remained trembled on their thrones. Nor was the *Papa-Re* immune to the general apprehension. As he regarded the gathering storm from his palace windows, Pius IX grew solemn, and began to regret his earlier reforms. A sign of his new mood was the appointment of the authoritarian Pellegrino Rossi as Prime Minister. It was not a popular move. On 16 November 1848, Rossi was assassinated as he arrived for work at the *Cancelleria*. A popular uprising was underway.

It is now that the Papal Zouaves begin to enter the picture. Living in Rome in 1848 was a former soldier turned priest, named Frederic Ghislain de Merode. Upon hearing of Rossi's assassination, Merode doffed his cassock and, armed to the teeth, hurried up to the Quirinal, where Pius IX was now besieged and offered to defend him against all comers. Pius decided that discretion was the better part of valour; he slipped away and took refuge with the King of Naples, at Gaeta. He remained in exile for just over a year, while a short-lived Roman republic was swiftly crushed by Neapolitan troops. Then the Pope returned, to rule as sovereign once again. But the time spent at Gaeta had not been fruitless. Firstly, Pius had spent much time in prayer before an image of the *Immaculata*, an altarpiece in the celebrated *capella d'Oro* on the seafront. His devotion to the sinless Virgin was to find expression in the dogmatic definition of the Immaculate Conception in 1854. But secondly, *Pio Nono*'s political outlook had undergone a rapid development – henceforth there would be no more flirtation with liberalism. The philosophical and theological roots of this liberalism were to be detailed and denounced in the famous *Syllabus Errorum* of 1864, but the Pope also looked around for more concrete ways of defending himself against the modern menace. In this context he remembered de Merode, realized he could trust him, and appointed him as 'Minister for War' to the Papal States.

The papal army over which de Merode assumed control was more a picturesque than a formidable fighting force. Swiss Guards, Noble Guards, Palatines and Grenadiers looked splendid on parade or doing guard duty at the Quirinal, but they were hardly a match for the far more modern forces that opposed them. It was the wealthy north of Italy, dominated by the Kingdom of Piedmont and its ruthless chancellor Cavour, which posed the biggest threat to the Papal States, and Piedmont had the money and resources to fund a large and professional army. De Merode needed help in creating some sort of similar force. He persuaded Pius IX to appoint General Louis La Morciere as Commander-in-Chief of the Papal Army, and actively to appeal to foreign volunteers to help defend the Papal States.

La Morciere, like de Merode himself, was a veteran of the French wars in Algeria, and it was he who chose the name 'Zouaves' for these foreign volunteers, taking the name from an Algerian light infantry corps. From the same source the Zouaves derived their slightly outlandish uniforms, which had a rather Middle Eastern look, including extremely baggy trousers. The first volunteers were French and Irish. Later, there arrived Belgians, unashamedly describing themselves as 'crusaders', and, as the fame of the Zouaves grew, so volunteers began to come from further and further afield. There were soon Zouaves from Holland, Scotland, Canada, Germany and (which is where Julian Watts-Russell enters our story) England.

The English and Welsh hierarchy had only just been restored (1850) and, encouraged by Cardinal Wiseman and Cardinal Manning, English Catholicism grew to have a markedly Ultramontane streak, devoted to the cause and person of the Holy Father and to the defence of his temporal sovereignty.[3] It is no surprise, therefore, that a large number of Englishmen joined the ranks of the Zouaves, and they soon formed a distinct section of the army. The

English Zouaves even had their own marching song, the first verse of which ran as follows:

> St George and old England for ever!
> Once more arm her sons for the fight!
> With the cross on their breasts to do battle,
> For God, Holy Church and the right!

There was also a special club for the English Zouaves in the heart of Rome, where they could smoke or play billiards in their off-duty hours, and of course they were always welcome guests at the *Venerabile*, where the Rector, Monsignor Neve, was a genial host, although he discouraged his own students from joining the corps.

In the memoirs of a certain Joseph Powell, one of these English Zouaves, we read of a day-trip to the old English College villa at Monte Porzio:

> We made two excursions to Monte Porzio, where the English College were staying for their *villeggiatura*. They received us, as usual, most kindly, and accompanied us part of the way back. We passed by the ruins of Tusculum ... On the site of the ruined city, a cross has been erected by the College and is visible for some miles.[4]

Powell also visited Palazzola (then still a Franciscan friary) and went with some other Zouaves to Nemi, where they enjoyed the strawberries and some local wine, which 'we pronounced excellent'.

But what of Julian Watts-Russell? Born on 6 January 1850, he was educated as a young man at Ushaw College, where he seems to have been of a somewhat pious disposition, but also pleasure-loving and active. At any rate, soon after leaving Ushaw in 1863 he took the decision to join the papal Zouaves, and hurried off to Italy to enlist. His elder brother, Wilfrid, accompanied him, and together they were enrolled in the papal Army.

During his military training, Julian combined the usual

life of a soldier (weapons drill, mock battles, bivouacs and manoeuvres) with outstanding prayer and devotion, attending daily Mass, saying his rosary every evening, and regularly confessing his sins. Such practices were by no means unusual among the Zouaves, who sincerely regarded themselves as crusaders against a tide of infidelity, and looked forward to a martyr's crown if they died in battle.[5]

A saying of Julian himself illustrates the point. Loading his gun one day, he remarked, as he pushed home the bullet, 'What a capital present that would be for Garibaldi!' 'Yes,' retorted a friend, 'but perhaps he may send you one instead.' 'So much the better,' replied Julian, 'for then I hope I should go straight to heaven.'

Julian's desire for an early death was to be granted him. On 2 November 1867 the Zouaves marched out to confront the Piedmontese forces at Mentana, a small town sixteen miles outside Rome on the banks of the Tiber.[6] In the ensuing battle, Julian displayed great courage as well as considerable charity, since whenever he fitted his gun he insisted on saying a 'Hail Mary' for whomsoever he might be dispatching into eternity. He himself died just outside the walls of Mentana. The papal forces were advancing successfully, and the enemy was compelled to give ground and fall back. As the Zouaves pushed forward, an enemy bullet struck Julian Watts-Russell in the eye, and he died immediately. When the battle was over (and the Piedmontese troops decisively defeated) three sisters of mercy collected Julian's body and sent it back to Rome, where it was buried with due honour in the cemetery of San Lorenzo. A little later, the monument, which today stands in the College church, was erected on the site where he fell.

How this monument came to find a home in the College requires some explanation. The first factor to be considered is the fall of the Papal States. Although they won the battle of Mentana, the Zouaves enjoyed very few military victories. Little by little the forces of a united Italy encroached upon what remained of the temporal power of the Pope and dealt his armies a series of humiliating defeats. Minister of War de Merode remained a favourite of Pius IX, but he was hated by the Pope's wily and unpleasant Secretary of State, Cardinal Antonelli (called, not without reason, 'the Italian Richelieu'). Antonelli eventually forced the resignations of both de Merode and General La Morciere, but the departure of these two hardly did anything to help the situation. Meanwhile, Antonelli himself was outmanoeuvred politically by the equally unsavoury Cavour, until at last nothing remained to safeguard papal Rome but the forebearance of the Piedmontese government. In 1864, having inflicted a series of crushing defeats on the Pope, Cavour agreed peace and undertook not to invade the City of Rome itself. This concession, however, was only made due to the presence in Rome of a garrison of French troops, placed there by Napoleon III in response to French Catholic sympathy for the besieged Pontiff. Cavour did not want to find himself fighting a war against France, and this alone forced him to bide his time. The outbreak of the Franco–Prussian war in 1870 provided him with the longed-for opportunity to invade. The Napoleonic garrison was withdrawn, and, regardless of the convention of 1864, the Piedmontese advanced. By now there was little to oppose their coming and they advanced through the environs of the city with ease. In the last days of papal Rome, a sharp-eyed student on the roof of the English College might have seen the white-clad figure of the Pope blessing the faithful from his balcony at the Vatican, while the white tents of the enemy were clearly visible on the surrounding hills.

The end came on 20 September 1870. The day before Pius IX had crossed Rome for the last time, travelling in his carriage from the Vatican to St John Lateran to review the troops drawn up in the piazza. Slowly the seventy-eight year old pontiff climbed the Scala Santa on his knees, then, at the top, he turned to bless the soldiers below him. It was his last act as king. At 5.15 the following morning the observatory of St Mary Major reported that the enemy had opened fire on the Tre Archi, Porta Maggiore and Porta Pia. At 5.55 a.m. the Vatican observatory noted intense fire between Porta Salaria and Porta S. Giovanni, and at 6.35 a.m. that firing had also begun between Villa Pamphilj and Porta S. Pancrazio. Around the Vatican the Swiss Guard and pontifical Gendarmes were drawn up before the Bronze Doors and all other entrances to the Apostolic Palace, in full battle array and apparently fearing attack.

Visitors began to arrive. Between 6.30 and 7.00 a.m. the entire Diplomatic Corps arrived, in gala carriages and full court dress, and alighted in the Cortile S. Damaso. They proceeded to hear the Pope's Mass, while meanwhile cannon thundered against the city walls, and grenades exploded on the Janiculum. The Pope, as was his custom, read his Mass rather slowly, seemingly oblivious to the crashes which were now shaking the glass in the windows and loggia of the palace. After Mass the Diplomatic Corps assembled before the Pontiff in his private library. Arnim, the Prussian representative, declared that those present would shield the Holy Father with their own persons if necessary. Pius responded that nothing of the sort should be necessary. He had already instructed his troops to offer only a token resistance, enough to protest at the illegality of the attack without the pointless squandering of lives. The Zouaves, however, and others in the papal Army, felt that their honour demanded more, and they proceeded to put up a stiff resistance. It was the Pope himself who intervened to put a stop to the bloodshed. At 9.30 a.m. he commanded a white flag to be raised from the *cupula* of St Peter's. The signal and its meaning were unmistakable. The papal forces, many of them in tears, laid down their arms and abandoned the hopeless struggle. By 10.00 a.m. firing had ceased throughout the entire city. The Patrimony of St Peter was no more.

For all the dire warnings of Cardinal Manning and others, the immediate effects of the fall of Rome were something of an anticlimax. The students of the English College, having prudently raised an enormous Union Flag over their property, took shelter in the cellars, where they were served with hot wine. The remaining Zouaves laid down their weapons in the gardens of the Doria-Pamphilj family, and marched out of Rome with full honours. Pius IX declared himself the 'Prisoner of the Vatican', and King Victor Emmanuel took up possession of the Quirinal. Rome's nobility divided itself into two camps, the 'black' (or clerical) party siding with the Pope and the 'white' favouring the new regime. In the black camp, strangely enough, was Victor Emmanuel's own daughter, Clotilde, who refused ever to visit her father in the Quirinal because she considered it to be stolen property. Even the king himself, it was said, could never bring himself to occupy the State Bedroom of the Sovereign Pontiff he had ousted. But whether one liked it or not, the facts were the same. The Popes' rule over Rome was now ended.

With the end of the temporal power, a certain reaction was inevitable, and one form this took was the vandalizing of monuments commemorating the old regime. One might think of the cross on Tusculum, visited by Joseph Powell and his fellow Zouaves in happier days and several times toppled by anticlerical malcontents about this time.[7] So it was that Julian Watts-Russell's monument at Mentana came to be toppled over and battered about, as we see it today, and eventually it was carted off to the cellars of a nearby *osteria*. There it might have lain to this day, had it not been for the enthusiasm of a certain English clergyman, who provides the most unusual element to our story.

Monsignor Claude Lindsay, an English priest living at S. Lorenzo in the 1890s happened to read the story of Julian Watts-Russell, and became convinced that his life had shown signs of heroic sanctity. He went out to Mentana, rescued the monument, and at his own expense had it re-erected in the church of the English College in 1895. However, his devotion to 'Julian, Saint and Martyr', as he referred to the Zouave, went still further. Unaccountably, he became convinced that Julian's body was incorruptible, and that, if his coffin was to be opened, the remains would be as fresh and whole as the day they were buried. So, at considerable trouble and expense, he set about trying to have the grave uncovered and the 'martyr's' relics exhumed. If this miracle were to be proved true, it would surely be the first step towards Julian's eventual elevation as a canonized saint of the Church. At last all his troubles were repaid, and he obtained permission for the grave to be opened. Alas for Monsignor Lindsay, however, nothing remained but a few bones, some shreds of cloth and a couple of buttons. The corpse itself had proved all too corruptible, and had decayed entirely. The good Monsignor gave up in despair, and never mentioned his erstwhile hero again.

But his enthusiasm did have one good result. The monument cast down at Mentana had found a safe and honourable resting place, and the memory of Julian Watts-Russell came to be preserved in the Venerable English College. Those who pass that monument today, so easily missed on the way into chapel, might do well to remember the forgotten byway of history it represents, and pause to remember the souls of all those who died in a doomed but noble cause.[8]

Notes

1. For the biographical details on Julian Watts-Russell I am indebted to James Johnson 'Julian Watts-Russell', in *The Venerabile*, vol. V (April 1932) 381–7, and the information supplied by Dr B. V. Miller for 'Nova et Vetera' in the same journal, vol. VI (October 1932). It should be noted that the *Scritture* in the College archive also contain various relevant documents, including letters belonging to Mgr. Stonor, chaplain to the English-speaking Zouaves.
2. Since this article was first published, Pius IX and John XXIII have been beatified at a joint ceremony in Rome, 3 September 2000.

3. It is worth noting that Cardinal Newman was always more sceptical about the benefits conferred by the temporal power – one of the factors which made him especially suspicious in the eyes of fervent *papalini* such as Manning and his ally Mgr. Talbot.
4. H. E. G. Rope, 'Joseph Powell, Pontifical Zouave', in *The Venerabile*, vol. IX, 229 (November 1939).
5. The Zouaves' antipathy to their contemporaries was entirely reciprocated, as F. M. Crawford noted. He calls the Zouaves 'the brave foreign legion enlisted under Pius the Ninth, in which men of all nations were enrolled under officers of the best blood in Europe, hated more especially by the revolutionaries because they were foreigners, and because their existence, therefore, showed a foreign sympathy with the temporal power, which was a denial of the revolutionary theory which asserted the Papacy to be without friends in Europe.' Francis Marion Crawford, *Ave Roma Immortalis*, London, second edition, 1928, pp. 509–10.
6. Mentana is today an entirely undistinguished spot, but was perhaps more famous in antiquity, since Hare notes that it is mentioned by Virgil, and its wines praised by Martial, Seneca and Pliny. Augustus Hare, *Days near Rome*, London, 1875, vol. I, p. 80.
7. See K. Haggerty, 'The English College and Tusculum, The Unfolding of Tradition', in *The Venerabile*, vol. XXIX, no. 4 (1990), 29–44. The present Tusculum cross was erected following the reconciliation of the Church with the State of Italy in 1929.
8. An impressive monument to the Zouaves of all nations stands in the Blessed Sacrament Chapel of St John Lateran. The nearby Lateran Historical Museum contains a number of Zouave uniforms and other memorabilia relating to the temporal power of the Papacy.

This article first appeared in the 1999 edition of 'The Venerabile'.

John Henry Newman and Ambrose St John in Rome, 1847.

John Henry Newman and the English College

Jerome Bertram, Cong. Orat.

When Newman and his pal Hurrell Froude stayed in Rome in spring 1833, they were both nervous of the city and its religion, terrified of priests, anxious about the fulfilment of apocalyptic prophecy. Was not this Rome, the Fourth Beast of the Prophet Daniel? Could they be sure the Beast was quite dead yet? 'And besides I cannot quite divest myself,' writes Newman, 'of the notion that Rome Christian is somehow under an especial shade as Rome Pagan certainly was – though I have seen nothing here to confirm it. Not that one can tolerate even for an instant the wretched perversion of the truth which is sanctified here ...'[1] Perhaps that is why it took them long to pluck up the courage to call on Dr Wiseman, and enter the terrifying portals of the English College. Although they had apparently tried to see him when they first arrived ('missed Dr Wiseman in the afternoon',[2] of 10 March), it was the Wednesday of Holy Week before they actually met him, Holy Saturday (6 April) before they had a chance to talk. Newman himself wrote little about the encounter: to Henry Jenkyn only, 'We have been to the English College here, which was founded in Saxon times – it was all but destroyed by the French, who behaved here (as everywhere) with the most brutish rapacity'.[3] To his sister

Jemima, he wrote, 'I ought to tell you ... about our communication with Dr Wiseman head of the English College ... Oh that Rome were not Rome; but I seem to see as clear as day that a union with her is *impossible*.'[4] For an explanation of the impossibility we have to turn to Froude, who described their conversation in greater depth: 'The only thing I can put my hand on as an acquisition is having formed an acquaintance with a man of some influence at Rome, Monsignor [Wiseman], the head of the [English] college, who has enlightened [Newman] and me on the subject of our relations to the Church of Rome. We got introduced to him to find out whether they would take us in on any terms to which we could twist our consciences, and we found to our dismay that not one step could be gained without swallowing the Council of Trent as a whole.'[5] Newman adds a note to the effect that he and Froude were not *genuinely* interested in reconciliation, Froude's words 'being a jesting way of stating to a friend what really was the fact, viz. that he and another availed themselves of the opportunity of meeting a learned Romanist to ascertain the ultimate points at issue between the churches'. Nevertheless, like many a prospective convert since, they do seem to have entertained the idea that a selection of Catholic doctrines could be mixed up to suit the English palate, safely leaving the full horrors of the Council of Trent for foreigners to enjoy.

When Newman took leave of Wiseman, the latter expressed a conventional wish to see him again. Newman demurred, saying he had a work to do in England. This presentiment of a work impending grew stronger during Newman's return to Sicily, and sustained him during his near-fatal illness there. 'I sat some time by the bedside, crying bitterly, and all I could say was, that I was sure God had some work for me to do in England.'[6] Froude had concluded his account of their visit to the English College, 'We mean to make as much as we can out of our acquaintance with Monsignor [Wiseman], who is really too nice a person to talk nonsense about.'[7] Wiseman could afford to bide his time: he would have much to do with Newman thirteen years later, but of Froude, alas, he saw no more.

When Newman returned to Rome, in the autumn of 1846, it was as a Catholic, enthusiastic for the faith, though still fastidious about the sanitary conditions, of Rome. Although he himself studied at Propaganda, he was a frequent visitor now to the English College. He was there for Christmas, 'where stopped for vespers', and returned on 30 December for 'theatricals and a supper'.[8] During the following spring he was a regular attender at theological debates, involving himself, Dr Ferdinand English, William Clifford, Thomas Grant the Rector, J. C. Shaw a student, and Ambrose St John. The subject was apparently the validity of Anglican orders, but there is no record of who spoke on which side.[9] He was evidently unhappy about some aspects of the College, for he wrote to F. S. Bowles on 21 February, 'I don't think the English College is the place for you, though it would take some time to give my reasons.' Nevertheless he remained on excellent terms with the College and its inmates, continuing to visit for dinner and even breakfast after he had moved to Santa Croce to begin his Oratorian life. After his ordination on 30 May (Trinity Sunday) he did not say his first Mass until 3 June, but on 5 June he celebrated his third 'at English College at St Thomas' altar ... we went to Palotti's for a reception.'[10] This was of course Saint Vincent Pallotti and his Congregation.

For most of the summer Newman stayed in Rome, calling on Wiseman who was staying at the College, and making plans for the establishment of the Oratory in England. In October he went for a short trip to the Castelli, and dined at the Villa in Monte Porzio with Dr Sharples and Dr Wells.[11] Finally, soon before leaving the City for the three-week journey to Birmingham, he took his leave of the English College on Monday 29 November 1847.[12] It was obviously during these many visits to the College, and while Newman was developing his ideas about the Oratory, that he heard the often-recounted story about St Philip Neri:

When the English College at Rome was set up by the solicitude of a great Pontiff in the beginning of England's sorrows, and missionaries were trained there for confessorship and martyrdom here, who was it that saluted the fair Saxon youths as they passed by him in the streets of the great city, with the salutation, *'Salvete flores martyrum'*? And when the time came for each in turn to leave that peaceful home, and to go forth to the conflict, to whom did they betake themselves before leaving Rome, to receive a blessing which might nerve them for their work? They went for a Saint's blessing; they went to a calm old man, who had never seen blood, except in penance; who had longed indeed to die for Christ, what time the great St Francis opened the way to the far East, but who had been fixed as if a sentinel in the holy city, and walked up and down for fifty years on one beat, while his brethren were in the battle. Oh! the fire of that heart, too great for its frail tenement, which tormented him to be kept at home when the whole Church was at war! and therefore came those bright-eyed strangers to him, ere they set out for the scene of their passion, that the full zeal and love pent up in that burning breast might find a vent, and flow over, from him who was kept at home, upon those who were to face the foe. Therefore one by one, each in his turn, those youthful soldiers came to the old man; and one by one they persevered and gained the crown and the palm, – all but one, who had not gone, and would not go, for the salutary blessing. My Fathers, my Brothers, the old man was my own St Philip.[13]

When Newman returned to Rome more than ten years later, much had changed. Instead of being the lionized and famous convert on whom the Pope and the hierarchy reposed such hopes, he came back in the depth of depression, crushed by the way in which the work he had been given to do by the Pope had been frustrated by the pride and inertia of Wiseman, and the racist hostility of Cullen.

He came briefly to Rome in the winter of 1856 in order to sort out difficulties between the Birmingham and London Oratories, and, in the course of a round of visits to canonists and dignitaries, found time for only one visit to the English College, on Sunday 27 January, when he dined, and preached.[14] A rare glimpse of him there is preserved in a rambling article by Donald Macleod, later Moderator of the Church of Scotland, writing twenty-seven years later:

> It was my good fortune to hear John Henry Newman preach in Rome. It was in the chapel of the English Roman Catholic College. I believe I was the only Protestant present, having gained admission through my friend, the Vice-Rector. The chapel was filled with English Romanists of all ranks and descriptions. Never will I forget the aspect of the preacher – that weird countenance of his – as he hurriedly entered from the sacristy, nor the intensity of his obeisance as he passed the altar on the way to the pulpit. It was not that he knelt, but that he seemed to crush himself down before it in brief, earnest prayer. His sermon was touching in the highest degree. Its theme was the experiences of St Paul on giving up all his former associations, beliefs, and friendships, in order to be true to his new convictions. As addressed by such a man to such an audience, the bearing of the discourse was obvious. More than once, as he read illustrative passages from the Acts and the Epistles, the half-suppressed sob showed how deeply the preacher was moved. However widely he might differ from Newman, his would have been a callous nature which could refuse its sympathy, or not feel all that was best in him quickened by the self-revelation given by this sincere and pure-hearted man.[15]

Ten years later the storm clouds were even darker over Newman's head, as a regular conspiracy of jealous clerics attempted to poison the ears of the pope against him.

Having succeeded in undermining the hopes of a Catholic University for the United Kingdom, they were now determined that Newman should not be allowed to encourage Catholics to go to any other university. The plans for the Oxford Oratory were so many times deferred or frustrated, that Newman sent Fr Henry Bittleston and Fr Ambrose St John to Rome to try to find out what was going on. He deluged them with telegrams and letters, using the English College as an address, though in the event the fathers stayed in an *albergo*. On 3 May 1867 they went to the College to see the Rector, Frederick Neve, who was consistently supportive of Newman and his friends. However they were elbowed out of the way by the unspeakable Monsignor Talbot, who 'kept them waiting no end of time'. Talbot afterwards cornered Fr Ambrose in the Vatican, alleging that he had not recognized them, but arguing fiercely against Newman's position. Blessed Pio Nono, on the other hand, was most friendly and helpful, so that Talbot changed tack and became affable, urging the Birmingham Fathers to dine with him.[16] Fr Ambrose for a moment agreed, but on thinking it over, sent the letter which survives in the College Archives. He had accepted Talbot's 'invitation for Fr Bittleston & myself to dine with you' but had reconsidered this in the light of their position 'as subjects of F. Newman acting in his name and in his behalf in a matter in which he feels with great justice he has been publicly wronged. We came because it was stated that he was persistently cooperating in a scheme of mixed education contrary to the express desire of the Holy See. The charge of disobedience in this matter I consider to have been sufficiently withdrawn' but he cannot accept 'hospitality from one who has before the world taken a strong line against him'.[17]

Talbot was not amused, and wreaked his vengeance by having Fr Neve turned out of his place as Rector of the English College.[18]

Newman's own final return to Rome had to wait until the ecclesiastical storm clouds were dispelled. The City had by now fallen to the barbarians, and it was a captive Pope who summoned Dr Newman to receive the Red Hat. Infuriatingly, the new Cardinal was confined to his rooms with a severe bout of influenza for virtually the whole of his stay in Rome, but he was able to visit the English College once, on 14 May 1879, when the English-speaking Catholics of Rome gave a reception for him and presented him with some vestments. This presentation had actually been arranged by Leo XIII himself: 'his kind interest extended so far as to settle the day, and the details of attendance, and of the Cardinal's dress for that day.'

> At eleven o'clock on Wednesday, *May* 14, his Eminence Cardinal Newman, accompanied by Mgr Cataldi, Master of Ceremonies to his Holiness, and the Fathers of the Birmingham Oratory who are with him, went to the English College to receive the address and the gifts of the English, Irish, Scotch and American residents in Rome. He was received at the College by Dr. O'Callaghan, the rector, Dr Giles, the vice-rector, and Mgr Stonor, and conducted to a large upper chamber, already crowded by ladies and gentlemen. At the further end were exposed the complete set of vestments, rich as becoming the intention, but plain in accordance with the Cardinal's desire, a cloth-of-silver cope and jewelled mitre, a Canon of the mass book, a pectoral cross and chain, and a silver gilt altar candlestick, for which the English-speaking Catholics at Rome have subscribed as a present to his Eminence, together with a richly illuminated address.

Lady Herbert of Lea read the address, and the Cardinal replied very briefly. He reflected that 'most men if they do any good die without knowing it; but I call it strange that I should be kept to my present age – an age beyond the age of most men – as if in order that, in this great city, where I am personally almost unknown, I might find kind friends to meet me with an affectionate welcome and to claim me as their spiritual benefactor.' The reporter notes that 'a great improvement was manifested in the Cardinal's appearance since the day before yesterday'.[19]

Fr Pope commented that 'He looked very noble in Cardinal's attire – and we sent to the Vatican for his *gentiluomo* in the picturesque mediaeval dress – with sword – and the Father's biretta on his knees. Two carriages and all in the proper form. But the Father is fearfully tired and weak. That grip on his throat and bronchia was a sharp one – and I shall be glad now to see him home again.'[20] In contrast, Fr Bacchus (who had been a student at the College) writes, 'the Father seemed to enjoy himself very much, laughing and making himself pleasant.'[21]

There, then, we may leave him in his glory, welcomed back in triumph in the College where he had first spoken to a Catholic priest forty-six years before, which he had frequently visited in the first months of *Pio Nono*, and where his envoys had been snubbed by the agents of the 'aggressive and insolent faction' who had made Newman's pilgrimage on earth a *via dolorosa* for so much of his life.

Notes

1. *Letters and Diaries* (LD) III, p. 258; letter of 18 March 1833 to R. F. Wilson.
2. LD III, p. 247.
3. LD III, p. 280.
4. LD III, p. 284.
5. J. H. Newman (ed.), *Remains of the late Reverend Richard Hurrell Froude, MA*, I, London 1838, pp. 306–7.
6. *Autobiographical Writings*, p. 136; cf. *Apologia*, p. 34.
7. *Remains*, I, p. 310.
8. LD XI, p. 302.
9. LD XII, pp. 16, 22, 27, 54, 57.
10. LD XII, p. 86.
11. LD XII, p. 124.
12. LD XII, p. 130.

13. 'The Second Spring', in *Occasional Sermons*, pp. 181–2.
14. LD XVII, p. 141.
15. 'Some Italian Memories, by the Editor', in Donald Macleod (ed.), *Good Words*, 1883, p. 424.
16. LD XXIII, p. 218.
17. Correspondence of Mgr George Talbot, indexed by Anthony Kenny, 1954, now classed as Libri 1635–1639, with index volume Liber 1640; letter 1164, 6 May 1867. The Talbot correspondence is most illuminative as to the extent of the machinations of Vaughan, Manning and party.
18. LD XXIII, p. 316.
19. The whole account of Newman's visit to the College is in W. P. Neville (ed.), *Addresses to Cardinal Newman with his Replies, etc. 1879–81*, London, 1905, pp. 71–4.
20. W. Ward, *The Life of John Henry Cardinal Newman*, II, 1912, p. 464.
21. LD XXIX, p. 125.

This article first appeared in the 2001 edition of 'The Venerabile'.

TRANSVERSE SECTION

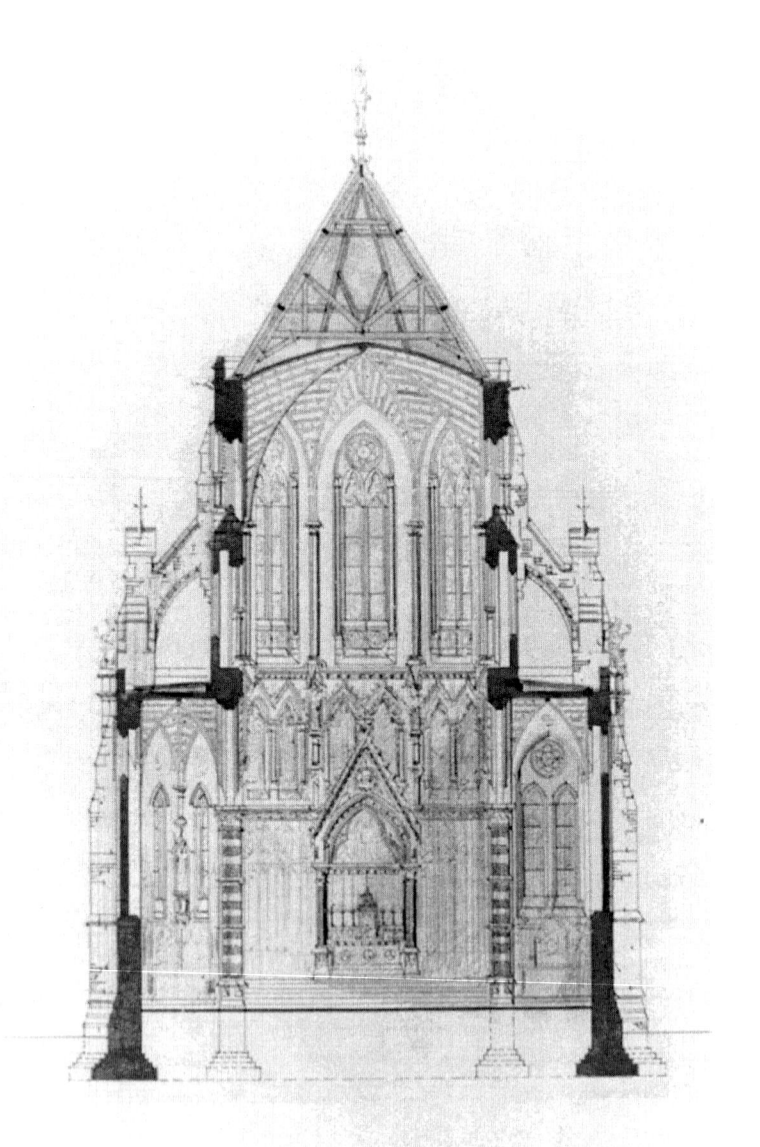

Edward Welby Pugin's 1864 neo-Gothic design for the College church

'Glorious Hopes and designs': The Pugins in Rome[1]

Carol Richardson

That the Gothic style of architecture stood for the continuity of the established Church of England through the Reformation, the medieval church and back to the apostolic succession was a basic premise of the Oxford Movement. However the appropriateness of the Gothic style relied not on its undeniably impressive possibilities, but on what revival meant.[2] Despite their common heritage as Anglicans who had converted to the Catholic faith, John Henry Newman and Augustus Welby Northmore Pugin responded very differently to the problem of finding an appropriate style of architecture for the building boom that accompanied Catholic emancipation and the restoration of the English Diocese in the middle of the nineteenth century. For Newman, Gothic became only a style that had in the past been appropriately used by the Church. For Pugin the Gothic style represented a great deal more. In 1848 Newman wrote to Ambrose Lisle Philips that, 'We know that the Church, while one and the same in doctrine ever, is ever modifying, adapting, varying her discipline and ritual. According to the times ... [Gothic] was once the prefect expression of the

Church's ritual in those places in which it was in use; it is not the perfect expression now'.[3] But what if an English Catholic church were to be built in Rome at the same time as the very concept of revival was being debated by both the Anglican and Roman churches in England? Should it be in the English or Roman style? This article examines exactly this scenario.

In 1847 A. W. N. Pugin visited Rome for the first and only time in his relatively short life. The reason for his visit remains a mystery though he clearly used it to renew acquaintances and extend contacts. On 24 April the architect dined with Philip Andrew, Prince Doria Pamphili.[4] Only a few weeks before, on 4 April, the prince had married Mary Alathea Beatrix, elder daughter of the Earl of Shrewsbury who had been Pugin's main patron since 1836.[5] Two days later Pugin met with John Henry Newman who had been resident at the College of the Sacred Congregation of the Propaganda since 1846.[6] Alexandra Wedgwood suggests that the two may have met to discuss Newman's plans for an Oratory, something that Pugin did not seem keen to do.[7] Then, on 1 May, the architect had the privilege of an audience with Pius IX, at which he gave the pope a specially bound edition of *Contrasts* and was given a gold medal. However, as quickly as possible after the audience, Pugin left the city and returned to England.

Pugin's haste to leave Rome was symptomatic of his uncompromising attitude to architecture. Indeed in architectural terms Pugin was appalled by the Eternal City, 'for every hour he was there he felt endangered his faith'.[8] If the architecture was bad (or rather, not Gothic) then religious and moral truth was absent.[9] 'Why they can't even carry out decently their own miserable style.'[10] Pugin's experience of Roman architecture perhaps marks his own naive devotion to the Gothic style as a very English response to a uniquely English set of circumstances. 'The modern churches here are frightful', Pugin wrote home from Rome.

St Peters is far more ugly than I expected, and vilely constructed – a mass of imposition – bad taste of every kind seems to have run riot in this place; one good effect however results from these abortions; I feel grateful for living in a country where the real glories of the Catholic art are being revived and appreciated. In Rome it is hopeless, unless by a miracle.[11]

What Augustus Welby did not live to see was that, through his son Edward, that miracle of reviving the 'real glories of the Catholic art' in Rome almost happened.

Any Englishman visiting Rome must have been affected by the dramatic contrast between the modest churches of Roman Catholics in England and those in Rome. Since the time of Henry VIII the Catholic community in England had been accustomed to making themselves as unobtrusive as possible. Indeed, as Roderick O'Donnell puts it, in England, 'Catholics called their churches chapels and built them accordingly'.[12] With the emancipation of the Catholic Church in England it was no longer necessary for those practising the Faith to hide in the background. For the first time in more than 300 years Catholics in England could openly celebrate their faith. However while what they were celebrating was not open to debate, in what style they should celebrate their English Catholicism was far more problematic.

To some, and in particular those who had been attached to the Oxford Movement since Keble's sermon in St Mary's Church on Sunday 14 July 1833, the Gothic style eloquently demonstrated the continuity of the True Church since the Gothic Middle Ages. John Henry Newman had once told a lecture audience: 'I think the Gothic style is endowed with a profound and commanding beauty such as no other style possesses with which we are all acquainted and which probably the church will not see surpassed till it attain to the Celestial City'.[13] Pugin could not have agreed more. Indeed at first both men had a great deal in common. Pugin had converted to the

Roman Catholic faith in 1835 and Newman ten years later in 1845 but Pugin did not see that the Gothic cause was not quite so straightforward for he died at the age of forty in 1852. Although in 1866, in his *Letter to Pusey*, Newman had made clear his preference for 'English habits of devotion to foreign', for him practical and spiritual necessity overruled such idealism.[14] Why should Catholic cathedrals be built when there were no bishops for them?[15] Increasingly for Newman the revival of Gothic architecture did not symbolize the Church rising like a phoenix out of the ashes of the Reformation, as it had done for Pugin, but was merely a form of escapism for those involved in it.

Opposition to the rising phoenix of the Roman Church in England was far less subtle beyond her fold. The publication of John Ruskin's *The Stones of Venice* in March 1851 was followed only three days later by the same author's pamphlet *Notes on the Construction of Sheepfolds*. Ruskin was keen to demonstrate that Protestantism in England was itself an active and dynamic force. Pugin had already been attacked for his efforts to identify the English Gothic Revival with the Oxford Movement and Catholic revival in an appendix to *The Stones of Venice*, 'Romanist Modern Art'.[16] The sheepfolds of Ruskin's pamphlet can be explained by George Croly, the Orange Irish clergyman, who wrote in 1849 of 'England, the Archiepiscopal Province of Rome!'

> Does not the blood of every man in England boil at the idea? England cut up into quarters like a sheep, for the provision of twelve Papists! England mapped out like a wilderness at the Antipodes, for the settlement of the paupers of Rome! England, the farm-yard of the 'lean kine' of Rome![17]

Obviously the search for an identity to mark the changed fortunes of the newly recognized Catholic Church in England was by no means as simple as the reclamation of the Medieval style from the Church of England established since Henry VIII. Instead an architectural identity had to represent the very different factions to be reconciled in the Church. 'English' or Irish Catholics, 'Old' Catholics, 'New' Catholics, 'verts', Ultramontanes, those from the north or south of the country – each represented a multitude of experience and expectation of the Roman Church. New Roman churches were required in England and Pugin was clear about what style they should be built in. However his experience on his visit to Rome reveals the very national nature of his experience of the Catholic Church. In Rome itself objections to the emancipation of the English Catholic Church and its apparent usurpation of the Gothic revival were not relevant. But what if an English church were to be built in Rome? What would the Gothic style represent there? We can examine exactly this scenario in an example which has been overlooked for its significance in the creation of an English Victorian Catholic identity. The whirlpool of interests and loyalties between the local church in England and the centrifugal force of Rome is represented by the contemporary rebuilding of a church for the English hospice and seminary in the city, the Venerable English College.

The missing link in the story of Pugin's visit to Rome, as it is in so much of English history since the fourteenth century, may very well be the Venerable English College. Having converted to the Catholic faith in 1835, Pugin had become part of the significant minority of English Catholics at an unprecedented moment in their turbulent history. The English College at Rome, established as a seminary in 1579 for the training of priests to send back to Protestant England, was part of the cultural landscape of the society he had entered. Since the fourteenth century it had been a hospice for pilgrims from England focused on the church of St Thomas of Canterbury, which had been added to the complex at the end of the fifteenth century. Many of the significant figures in the re-establishment of the Roman hierarchy in England in 1850 came through the *Venerabile*. For example, Nicholas Wiseman and Daniel Rock had entered the English College at Rome as students in December 1818.[18] In 1828 Wiseman had become Rector of the College. Wiseman and Pugin had come across one another on several occasions, including the consecration of St Chad's Cathedral, Birmingham.[19] Rock was ordained in 1824 and served as chaplain from 1827–40 to Lord Shrewsbury, Pugin's patron. Indeed the chaplain and the architect met in 1836–7 when Pugin was probably making illustrations for Rock's book *The Church of Our Fathers*.

In this context it is unimaginable that Pugin would not have had some knowledge of or contact with the *Venerabile* while he was in Rome, and would have been aware of the plight the College was suffering at the time. On 27 July 1819 work had begun on demolishing the old church of the English College. This was not in preparation for a new building scheme but a desperate response to the predicament of the few years before. In 1798 the College had been emptied of its staff and students when Napoleon Bonaparte's army entered Rome under General Berthier. The French used the College buildings as a barracks and the church to stable their horses. The wood of the College roof and the trees in the garden seem to have been used to repair and heat the buildings during the French occupation. By the time of the Apostolic Visit of 1824 the English College church no longer existed.[20] Even by the time of Pugin's death in 1852 there was no church at the College nor was one planned until, in 1864, Edward Welby Pugin, the elder son who was 'brought up in his father's office', was asked to submit plans for a new national church in Rome.[21]

Pugin's first son, Edward Welby, was born in 1834 to Louisa, his second wife. Only 16 when his father died in 1852, he took over his father's practice and completed some of his work, including St Augustine's, Ramsgate. Known mainly as a church architect, like his father, Edward was an uncompromising and incessant worker who was often involved in disputes and his patrons, and as his contact with the English College in Rome confirms. In 1875 he died at the age of only forty-one, after a busy morning's work and an afternoon in a Turkish bath in Buckingham Palace Road, London.[22]

The Pugins' contact with Rome is a significant moment in the creation and definition of an English Roman Catholic identity. The English College found itself never far from controversy of preparing English priests for English ministry as far away as Rome. The 1770s in Rome had seen the suppression of the Society of Jesus, which had since Gregory XIII (1572–85) plugged the gap left by the Reformation in the training of priests to send back to Protestant nations. Italian staff had taken over running the English College but were not equipped to do so. The students complained of the illogicality of being prepared to preach in England by being only allowed to use Italian and Latin during their time in Rome, for 'the first thing required for a Preacher is the knowledge of the Language he has to preach in ... Who can here look at our preachings, correct them, show us the inaccuracies?'[23] With the restoration of the English hierarchy there was a strong case for the redefinition of the *Venerabile*'s role. Some, including the Jesuits at Stonyhurst, believed that a seminary in Rome was no longer necessary.[24] However, in some quarters at least, the building of an English College church in Rome was a national duty:

> ... no appeal has, in fact, been ever made to English Catholics which is more strictly national in its character, and which should properly enlist the sympathies of the English people. There is not a Catholic on the face of the earth who does not instinctively turn to Rome as his home – as the centre from which emanate unity, strength, and peace, like the rays from the summer's sun.[25]

The correspondence between the younger Pugin and the English College covers the period from 7 April, 1864, when the architect was about to leave Ramsgate for Rome, to 2 March 1874 when settlement was finally reached between the parties. The correspondence between Pugin and the English party in Rome features the chief representatives of English Catholicism there, among them Monsignor George Talbot, confidential adviser to the pope on English affairs, fifth son of Lord Talbot of Malahide, convert to the Catholic faith since 1846 and vehement supporter of *Roman* Catholicism: the rebuilding of the English College church was clearly of significance beyond the confines of the seminary. The negotiation between Rome and the younger Pugin is a unique and impassioned dialogue of principle over compromise. The high values espoused by the Gothic cause had to be balanced with the severe pressures – political and financial – suffered throughout the newly recognized Church. In this respect, the story of the Pugin firm's contact with the Venerable English College is a telling case study of a defining era in English religious and architectural history.

In his first letter to the English College, at the same time as announcing his site visit to Rome, the architect made clear the principles that he hoped would inform his plan. An English church, even one far away in Rome, should be in the English i.e. Gothic style, not the Italian. In this Edward Welby Pugin proved himself to be his father's son:

> ... the English Church should rather be in the distinctive marks of our own style of Gothic, of course as applied to the requirements of the Country rather than follow the Italian type. I imagine the windows might be fewer in number and smaller in size than in our own northern climate, but even this individuality may be in a great measure met by filling the windows with deep stained glass. The heat being kept but by means of double glazing.[26]

A. W. N. Pugin's thesis that a building should be true to its place and true to local materials obviously informed Edward's initial response to the commission.[27] In the very different Italian context, unaltered English solutions would not be appropriate: less wall space given up to windows would keep the building cooler in the Roman sun and warmer in the winter. Double glazing or darkly coloured stained glass – an obviously Gothic touch – would have the same effect. There was no question that the new church would be in anything but the Gothic style. That the local style of Rome was not Gothic did not seem to worry either father or son. Augustus was disgusted at the architectural style of the city while to Edward an English church, even one in Italy, should be Gothic – truth to local traditions and materials meant truth to *English* traditions and materials.

The plans submitted by Edward to the College are highly worked drawings. They clearly indicate in some detail that this was to be a richly coloured and ornamented edifice, something more typical of Edward's practice than of his father's: 'fussiness was, of course, the curse of E. W. Pugin ... yet it is undeniably splendid'.[28] The site left vacant was by all accounts the only constraint to the Gothic vision, being strictly limited by College buildings on either side. However this was something that Edward had already encountered at the Church of Saints Peter and Paul, Cork (1859–66).[29] The rounded apse would also have created an exterior space, abutting the street on one side and closed on the other by the sacristy. (In another plan for the same site this plot is clearly intended as a garden with trees and railings.) Underneath the church was to be a crypt on the same ground plan but with a lower arcade. This would have suited the site, with its deep foundations made necessary by the Roman soil, and the long history of eminent burials at the College.[30] Buttresses along the nave and around the apse are emphasized at every opportunity by pinnacles of angels, the largest rising above the apse itself. Both inside and out sculpted figures – presumably prophets and saints – decorate the wall spaces, standing on brackets in spandrels. Throughout, the building was obviously to be richly decorated with every available material: stone, wood and ironwork.

The west end of the church is marked by a tower and bellcote, incorporating the main access into the space. However missing on the plans is the solution to the problem of the west end which would have abutted the College buildings and thus remained windowless. This problem would have been solved in part in the interior by the dramatic distraction of the lighting of the east end.

Edward's greatest achievement in architecture – his union of the Gothic Revival with the Counter-Reformation apsed basilica – is clearly shown in the plans.[31] There is no sign of Augustus Welby's square-ended east ends which intentionally followed the English regional Gothic style. Instead an ornamented exterior outside and dramatic lighting inside emphasize this focus on the canopied altar and sanctuary, reflecting Tridentine reference to the visibility of the sanctuary and altar. Three tall windows would have contrasted the relatively bright chancel with the rest of the dark building, leading into the choir and on down into the nave. The three layers of aisle, triforium and clerestory are each broken by windows. However the windows on the arcade and triforium levels would presumably have contained stained glass set within heavy traceries. The brightest light would have come from the round windows surmounting each bay which would have lit the vault and sent a diffused light into the nave.

The practical purpose of the church divided the plan into three distinct zones of sanctuary, choir and nave. The choir for the members of the College community, and the nave for the parish of English Catholics in Rome, occupy equal parts of the long, thin church. Steps between the nave and choir emphasize the hierarchical arrangement of the space and, combined with the brighter lighting of the apse, further emphasize the chancel. As well as the high altar, the plans include four side altars, two at the east end of the aisles and two piercing the north wall. These parts of the space are united once more by the eight-bayed arcade and stone cross-vault, suspended from a steep pitched roof.

Edward Pugin's visit to Rome seems to have been a tremendous success for he returned to Ramsgate not only to carry out designs but also to raise money for the commission. On 27 May, almost as soon as the younger Pugin had returned from Rome, the architect wrote to thank Monsignor Talbot for his hospitality on his visit, and to press the continuance of the cause he was obviously enthusiastically supporting in every way. Edward reported that he was making progress in ensuring subscriptions for the project and pressed the College to publish a list, headed by the pope, as 'on this list will depend the position which the matter will take in the view of the Public ... do an immensity of good and crush all opposition'.[32] Progress with the plan and financing it was obviously not altogether taken for granted as this last point suggests. Indeed, the next letter from Pugin to the English College makes it clear that not all was well. The plans for the church had to be reduced: 'The Church is now in hand, and I trust will turn out to be, one of the most successful, as well as being one of the cheapest Churches ever built. I hope to forward Dr Neve my reduced plans for St Thomas's towards the end of next week'.[33] But the same letter also suggests that the Pugin firm was experiencing some problems in public relations of its own. Talbot, the papal secretary and English agent in Rome, had become arbitrator in a disagreement between Goldie and Pugin concerning the construction of a church in Kensington for the Carmelite community there. The building boom was clearly not without its problems.

The means of raising money for the new church was itself a huge task. Talbot spent long months in England going round the English Catholic community, promoting the scheme and searching for subscribers to it. Talbot's appearance in so much of the business of rebuilding the

English College Church accords with contemporary impressions of him as 'a well-meaning, fussy man ... of almost childlike simplicity, with a love of managing things and persons, from the Pope downwards'.[34] However Talbot found on his travels that the changed fortunes of the Church were not to everyone's liking:

> They [the laity] are jealous of the independence of the clergy. Up to this time the clergy have been servants of the laity, now they are coming out and asserting their Independence which they do not like. Nevertheless, I intend to fight them, and the Archbishop is equally well disposed.[35]

As well as Talbot's journeys round the country to promote the cause of the English College, pamphlets and subscription lists were circulated. In 1868 the case was presented and progress reported as follows:

> It is now two years since an appeal was made to the Catholics of England, on behalf of our National Church of S Thomas of Canterbury, in Rome.
> Since then the works have never been interrupted, although as yet not much is to be seen above ground. Owing to the peculiar character of the Roman soil, which is loose earth accumulated during two thousand years, we have been obliged to spend much time and money on five lines of foundations, nearly fifty feet deep, and on other preliminaries to prepare the site.
> Now happily the foundations are completed, and we have begun to put in their site the marble bases, to erect the columns, and to build the walls. Our Architect promises that before next Feast of St Thomas, five columns shall be erected, and the walls raised to the height of twelve feet, so that we hope to have some progress to show to the assembled Bishops at the opening of the Œcumenical Council.
> The Holy Father has conferred on the English Nation

the great honour of laying the First Stone two years ago, so that the work was commenced under the highest auspices ... The sum is not great we require to complete the Church. We therefore fervently pray all the English Catholics who have not yet subscribed to respond to this appeal ...[36]

Subscriptions were made, from £150 from Cardinal Wiseman, the aged Archbishop of Westminster, £100 from The Duchess of Hamilton (the Hamiltons being the second Roman Catholic family of Scotland after the Stuarts), to two shillings from 'A Poor Man Leicester'. Even the French national church in Rome, San Luigi dei Francesi contributed with a donation of £5. However donations came in slowly and not everyone supported the cause with there being so much building work needing finance in England itself.[37]

By 1867, however, Edward Pugin's part in the rebuilding of the English College church in Rome was over. In October he wrote what was obviously not the first letter asking for a settlement: 'I have written such times both to yourself and to Mon. Neve respecting a settlement in one form or other of my claim to St Thomas's Church in Rome, as no attention has been paid to my proposition I now have to forward my a/c and should be glad to receive then a cheque for the same at your early convenience'.[38] Indeed Pugin made it clear that the way he had been treated by the English College was 'thoroughly unsatisfactory ... But although I feel deeply aggrieved at the manner in which I was treated, I have no wish to insist upon my legal rights, but I should be glad to have the matter fairly and finally settled without delay'.[39] These legal rights entitled him to $3^{1}/_{2}\%$ of the original commission which he duly reduced to $2^{1}/_{2}\%$ plus expenses, a total of £350 minus £25 donation to the appeal he had been working for.

Perhaps the only reason that the plans for the Pugin church have survived at all is due to the vision of the architect. In 1868 Talbot wrote to Henry O'Callaghan, recently appointed as the new Rector of the English College after Frederick Neve, of the latest development:

> After a considerable deal of consideration I have made an offer to Pugin of £100 now and another £100 within five years. As yet he has not accepted. Nevertheless he is finishing his designs as he wishes them always to remain in the English College. This I have promised him would be the case. They will be beautiful.[40]

By May 1867 another architect, but this time an Italian, Count Virginio Vespignani, was well under away with the task of building the church.[41] However even this scheme was not straightforward. It was dogged by financial problems and work halted not least because of the depth of the foundations necessary in that part of the city near the river. Nevertheless, in July 1868, Vespignani wrote that the church would be able to open to the public in 1870 'sotto gli occhi dell'Episcopato Cattolico riunito ancora nel Concilio Ecumenico.'[42] Pugin was appalled by the plans which had replaced his own:

> I have just seen the designs of the architect who succeeded me. I should not hesitate in saying that such a change is a disgrace to everyone concerned. The design is utterly worthless in every respect ... but the work of the *signore* the professional gentleman in question, not only in your case, but in anything he has touched, shows a wealth of decadence which can only be described as deplorable./ If my work had been replaced by something more worthy of the occasion, I should have had but small right to complain, but when I was for what thanks been set aside, I can no longer repress my indignation, not only on account of myself but on account of the causes./ If the building is like the view, it is not a Church and it does not even pretend to be a collegiate chapel. I now enter my protest against it, nobody will deny many a vigorous line about it./ What

single characteristic mark has it to show its origin?/ ... I have been most shamefully treated in this matter, but whatever the treatment has been towards myself personally it has been more towards that of the College and the cause.[43]

But why was Edward Pugin dropped as architect of the new English College Church when at the start all sides had seemed so enthusiastic? Edward spent another five years searching in vain for a clear answer to this question. He clearly felt aggrieved in the way he had been treated. Having lost the commission for the College he had been bought off with the promise of another but this did not come to anything:

> ... you are perfect in your impression that I intend to act generously towards you, but I should certainly expect a quid pro quo in your acting fairly towards me./ I will here remark that Cardinal Wiseman on several occasions promised that I should be the architect of the Westminster Cathedral whenever it was erected, and on the occasion when staying here, His Eminence said, 'In return I shall expect you will do your best with Sir John Sutton to obtain me a site'. I performed my part of the bargain, but I now learn that Archbishop Manning has given the intended work to Mr Clutton, This I consider simply unjust, and such I believe is the opinion of almost everyone. This is my statement and I believe you will find it consistent in every particular.[44]

Without a satisfactory explanation Pugin decided that his loss of the contract was due to the personalities involved:

> From all I hear I firmly believe that the Archbishop has been in this, as well as in everything else my unrelenting enemy, and probably the principal cause of my not having the work./ I wish you could discover and let me know the cause of this extraordinary persecution.[45]

Edward had been convinced in London that Archbishop Manning deliberately excluded him, probably because of his loyalty to Rome and the Roman style. In 1862 Pugin had had occasion to write to Cardinal Wiseman about the negative influence of 'Dr Manning and the Bayswater clique' on his career.[46] Manning, by all accounts, owed his career in the Roman church to his ability to make such associations, something he did with consummate skill in Rome.[47] Indeed it must have been quite a blow for the Gothic cause when Cardinal Wiseman died in February 1865, less than a year after Pugin's first involvement with the cause to rebuild the English College church. However these problems of the association of style with particular ideological camps went back to his father's promotion of the Gothic style. Indeed Edward Pugin's business was clearly identified with that of his father, Augustus. In claiming just compensation for his loss of the English College commission, Talbot had quoted his father's work on the Houses of Parliament back at him: 'you [Talbot] state that my father only received £400 for the designs of the Houses of Parliament, but you forget that Barry the ostensible architect pretty well £200,000'.[48] Talbot, who was not renowned for his tact, may not have been aware of the animosity between Edward Pugin and Barry: Pugin had published a pamphlet just after Barry's death in which he claimed that it was his father who had been responsible for the success of that particular building.[49]

In the end the younger Pugin seems to have concluded that the problem lay in the nationalities involved. In Rome, Roman, not English precedents and preferences mattered: 'I firmly believe that this matter has caused you as much pain as myself and that you have had no other alternative than to comply with the wishes of Cardinal Antonelli and the Roman authorities', Pugin wrote in July 1868.[50] The architect may well have been correct in his detection of interference from Rome. As Papal Secretary of State Cardinal Antonelli was the senior member of the College, and as such had advised Cardinal Wiseman to be wary of auspicious display that would antagonize the English Protestants.[51] In September 1868 Talbot, a passionate Ultramontane and thus on the side of the ecclesiastical authorities in Rome, tried to bring the affair to a close – 'the reason why you could not be employed as architect was that I mentioned to you when we met at Hanover Lodge. The Archbishop had nothing to do with the decision. Circumstances obliged us in Rome to come to it, which I alluded to in our conversation'.[52] In the mind of the Roman authorities the problem was more financial than personal. But the affair was by no means over and the different personalities involved do not seem to have helped hasten the matter to a satisfactory conclusion. By 1873 Pugin had still not received compensation; Henry O'Callaghan was Rector of the College, William Giles the Vice-Rector and the church project in the hands of the Italian authorities under Monsignor Vitelleschi.

In July 1873 Giles visited Pugin, 'who was very civil', to prove his claim for compensation as promised by Talbot.[53] Only in February 1874 did Pugin finally receive the money promised him despite the financial difficulties the College found itself in.[54] In the end the church of the English College was only completed in 1888, almost twenty years after the Vatican council. Vespignani's finished building was judged a compromise between old and new by Cardinal Newman, according to whom 'the unsightly shell of a thoroughly modern Church was substituted for the old basilica under the direction of Valadier, a good architect, but one who knew nothing of the feelings which should have guided his mind and pencil in such work'.[55]

The whole scheme seems to have started as a compromise, something that Edward Pugin does not seem to have been ready to accept at any stage. In fact the 1860s saw four plans for four very different churches being drawn up for the site including a 'Roman Medieval Church', complete with coffered ceiling inside and iron railings outside (a most un-Italian detail). Even Vespignani's plan was not executed in full with the curved apse being substituted for a flattened east end abutting rather than destroying the neighbouring buildings, as any apse would have necessitated.

Ironically the restoration of the English hierarchy compromised the national character of the Church, as defined by the Pugins, rather than promoting it. As part of an international Catholic community, the way was open for international influences in England over local ones. The maintenance of local identity, such as available through Pugin's Gothic vision, required insularity. As it had been for his father Augustus Northmore, so it was for Edward Welby Pugin. Edward had found his contact with Rome distasteful. In his final letter to the English College he bitterly concluded:

> For my part I always thought I said that building the Church of St Thomas of Canterbury at Rome was a mistake. What was the use of building the 366th church in Rome? The true thing would have been, to have sold off the property and have founded a College in England.[56]

Religious reform did not lead to the better architecture and better society that the Pugins sought: even religious reform cannot be separated from the social and cultural context. The process of the emancipation of English Catholics incorporated an international social and cultural heritage rooted in Rome. The rebuilding of the church of St Thomas of Canterbury at the Venerable English College in Rome, at so crucial a juncture in the development of English cultural identity, makes this particularly clear.

Notes

1. Archives of the Venerable English College, Rome (hereafter VEC), *Scritture* 81:4–2.
2. Michael Hall, 'What Do Victorian Churches Mean? Symbolism and Sacramentalism in Anglican Church Architecture,

1850–1870', *JSAH* 59:1 (March 2000), 78–80.
3. Newman to Philips, 15 June 1848, in C. S. Dessain, (ed.), *The Letters and Diaries of John Henry Newman*, XII, London, 1962, p. 221, quoted in Hall, ibid., 80.
4. Alexandra Wedgwood, *AWN Pugin and the Pugin Family: Catalogues of Architectural Drawings in the Victoria and Albert Museum*, V&A Museum, London, 1985, p. 82 n.2.
5. Michael Trappes-Lomax, *Pugin: A Mediæval Victorian*, London, 1932, pp. 97–119; Margaret Belcher, *AWN Pugin: An annotated critical bibliography*, London and New York, 1987, p. 478.
6. Brian Martin, *John Henry Newman, His Life and Work*, New York, 1982, pp. 79–84.
7. Wedgwood, *Catalogues*, 94 n.9: Newman later recorded that Pugin 'implied that he would as soon build a mechanics' institute as an oratory'.
8. Benjamin Ferrey, *Recollections of AWN Pugin and his Father Augustus Pugin*, first published 1861, London, 1978 edition with an introduction by Clive Wainwright, p. 151.
9. Andrew Saint, 'The Fate of Pugin's True Principles', *Pugin: A Gothic Passion*, Paul Atterbury and Clive Wainwright (eds), New Haven and London, 1994, p. 273.
10. Ferrey, *Recollections*, p. 151.
11. Wainwright, 'Pugin and his Influence', *Pugin: A Gothic Passion*, 8: 'When Pugin was in Dorsetshire, engaged in rebuilding a chancel and parsonage, a friend started him upon a subject on which he knew that Pugin felt very uneasy just then, viz. The Italian taste that was rife amongst the Roman Catholics in England. To the utter bewilderment of those present he began vehemently to denounce the Romanizers; and, a well-known name in the Anglo-Roman hierarchy being mentioned as one of them, he exclaimed: "Miserable! My dear sir, miserable!" The clergyman for whom he was building, who at that time was more than half inclined to think everything Roman must be right, was utterly astonished to hear so distinguished a convert giving vent to such heresies; and his friend had to explain that the heresy was on the other side, but that it was only architectural.' Ferrey, 161, 225–6.
12. Roderick O'Donnell, 'Pugin as a Church Architect', *Pugin: A Gothic Passion*, p. 63.

13. A. N. Wilson, *Eminent Victorians*, London, 1989, p. 141.
14. Martin, *Newman, His Life and Work*, p. 118.
15. O'Donnell, 'Pugin as a Church Architect', *Pugin: A Gothic Passion*, p. 63 n.5.
16. Tim Hilton, *Ruskin: The Early Years*, New Haven and London, 1985–2000 edition, p. 149.
17. Quoted in Hilton ibid., pp. 149–50.
18. VEC *Liber Ruber*, 1818–1919.
19. Phoebe Stanton, *Pugin*, London, 1971, pp. 48–9, 66, 79–80.
20. VEC *Scritture* 61:1: Relazione o sia Foglio di Risposte alle dimande transmesse dalla Sagra Visita Apostolica il 26 Giugno 1824. La Chiesa publica col Cemeterio più non esiste, essendo rimasta soppressa sin dall'Anno 1787, perchè minacciava ruina, e dipoi descrata, e distrutta l'oggetto della sua instituzione nell'Anno 1351 fu' per servire all'Ospedale ed Ospizio dei Pellegrini Inglesi, fintanto che nel 1579 l'Ospedale, ed Ospizio furono dal Papa Gregorio XIII convertiti in un Collegio per l'educazione del Clero d'Inghilterra.
    Nel 1820 sono state riedificate da fondamenti le Mura, ed il tetto per la conservazione di detta Chiesa, che forma corpo con il Fabbricato del Collegio situato in Via di Monserrato Numero 45, a per manianza di fondi non si è potuta completare. Attese le note passate vicende non si è possuto ricuperare di detta Chiesa, che un Quadro rappresentante la Ssma Trinità dipinto da Durante Alberti, ed un Deposito di Marmo del fa Cavaliere Dereham Fatto da Pietro della Valle, che si conservano nel Collegio.
21. Roderick O'Donnell, 'The Later Pugins', *Pugin: A Gothic Passion*, p. 259.
22. Roderick O'Donnell's study of nineteenth-century church architecture includes the most useful of very few mentions of Edward Pugin. See his essays in *AWN Pugin: Master of Gothic Revival* and *Pugin: A Gothic Passion*.
23. VEC *Liber* 815, Diary of Rev'd John Kirk, 1773–1779, pp. 128–9.
24. VEC *Scritture* 71:10 'Jesuit Affairs' (Stonyhurst Scheming against VEC 1810–1875).
25. VEC *Scritture* 82:3 Lady Fitzherbert of Lea's response to the 1868 appeal.
26. VEC *Scritture* 81:4–1 Ramsgate 7 April 1864.

27. See Stanton, *Pugin*, p. 81 for a discussion of these principles.
28. Nicholas Pevsner, *Buildings of England: South Lancashire*, pp. 74–5 (quoted in O'Donnell, 'The Later Pugins', *Pugin: A Gothic Passion*, p. 267).
29. O'Donnell, 'The Pugins in Ireland', *AWN Pugin*, p. 155.
30. The burials at the College had been thrown into disarray by two episodes: the collapse of the College church's floor in 1687 and the French occupation in the 1790s (*Scritture* 81:2–24). Pugin's crypt would have allowed plenty of space for appropriate reorganization of these relics of the College's past.
31. O'Donnell, 'The Later Pugins', *Pugin: A Gothic Passion*, p. 265.
32. VEC *Scritture* 81:4–2, Edward Pugin to Talbot.
33 VEC *Scritture* 81:4–3, Edward Pugin to Talbot dated 31 May 1865. Monsignor Frederick Neve was Rector of the English College from 1863 to 1868.
34. Dom Cuthbert Butler, *Life and Times of Bishop Ullathorne*, London, 1926, vol. I, p. 227.
35. VEC *Scritture* 81:4–8 Talbot to O'Callaghan 2 July 1868, Hanover Lodge. In 1867 Talbot had expressed similar views on lay involvement in the administration of the church: 'What is the province of the laity? To hunt, to shoot, to entertain? These matters they understand, but to meddle with ecclesiastical matters they have no right at all'. Quoted in Edward Norman, *The English Catholic Community in the Nineteenth Century*, Oxford, 1984, p. 24.
36. VEC *Scritture* 82:3.
37. Cardinal Gasquet, *A History of the Venerable English College, Rome*, London, 1920, p. 265.
38. VEC *Scritture* 81:4–4, Edward Pugin to Talbot dated 30 October 1867.
39. VEC *Scritture* 81:4–6, Pugin to Talbot Ramsgate, 8 April 1868.
40. VEC *Scritture* 81:5–11, Talbot to O'Callaghan dated 18 July 1868.
41. VEC *Scritture* 81:6, Vespignani to Talbot dated 10 May 1867.
42. VEC *Scritture* 81:6, Vespignani to Talbot dated July 1867.
43. VEC *Scritture* 81:4–9, Pugin to Talbot Ramsgate 21 July 1868.
44. VEC *Scritture* 81:4–5, Pugin to Talbot Ramsgate 24 October 1867.

45. VEC *Scritture* 81:5–12, Pugin to Talbot Ramsgate 4 September 1868.
46. Archdiocese of Westminster, Wiseman papers W3/52/55, Pugin to Wiseman, 26 February 1862, quoted in O'Donnell, 'Later Pugins', *Pugin: A Gothic Passion*, p. 262.
47. Norman, *The English Catholic Community in the Nineteenth Century*, pp. 258–9.
48. VEC *Scritture* 81:4–5, Ramsgate 24 October 1867.
49. Kenneth Clarke, *Gothic Revival*, p. 162. Alexandra Wedgwood, 'The New Palace of Westminster', *Pugin: A Gothic Passion*, pp. 219–36; on Talbot's character in administration see Brian Fothergill, *Nicholas Wiseman*, London, 1963, p. 286.
50. VEC *Scritture* 81:4–9, Ramsgate 21 July 1868.
51. Holmes, *More Roman than Rome: English Catholicism in the Nineteenth Century*, London, 1978, 87; Norman 118.
52. VEC *Scritture* 81:5–13, 5 September 1868.
53. VEC *Scritture* 81:5–17, 19 July 1873.
54. VEC *Scritture* 81:5–21, 2 March 1874.
55. Quoted in Joseph Cartmell, 'The Church of St Thomas of the English', *Venerabile*, vol. III, no. 1, October 1926, p. 39.
56. VEC *Scritture* 81:5–20, Pugin to O'Callaghan, dated 2 March 1874.

This article was originally included in the 2000 edition of 'The Venerabile'.

Cardinal Edward Howard.

Memories of a Victorian Cardinal: Edward Howard

Abbot Sir David Oswald Hunter-Blair, O.S.B.

I was presented to Edward Archbishop Howard in the spring of 1875, soon after my reception into Holy Church, and have many recollections of his kindness to me, both before and after his elevation to the cardinalate. He was at that time in the prime of life, about forty-five; and I well recollect his tall, burly form, handsome ruddy features, and military carriage (it was almost a swing), recalling his service in Her Majesty's Life Guards, before he entered the priesthood. I think his last military duty had been to ride with his troop at the head of the great procession at the Duke of Wellington's funeral. He had been ordained on the great day (8 December 1854) of the Definition of the Immaculate Conception; and much of his life, as a simple priest, had been devoted to the service of the sick poor of Rome, towards whom his zeal and charity never flagged.

I had the honour of receiving confirmation at the Archbishop's hands, and of dining with him on the same day at his beautiful residence, the Villa Negroni, in the new quarter of Rome (a district not in favour with the *Papalini*, who nicknamed it *Buzurropolis*). He was an accomplished linguist as well as a most agreeable host; and nothing pleased him more than to preside at his own table, supported, perhaps, on either side by a Greek Patriarch and a Spanish Archbishop, with a French royalist marquis opposite and a couple of English *monsignori* round the corner. After his elevation to the cardinalate he, though personally of simple tastes, kept up considerably more state than his Roman colleagues. Subsequent to the Occupation of Rome by the Italians in 1870, the Cardinals had, by the Pope's wish, abandoned the use of their famous gilt and bedizened coaches, and drove about in lamentable-looking black carriages, drawn as a rule by the sorriest of steeds. Even when they took their walks at the back of the Pincian Hill (their favourite promenade) they were supposed to dispense with all insignia of their rank, and to go habited as simple priests.

Cardinal Howard did not pay very much regard to these conventional sumptuary regulations. He went out for his drives, not, certainly, in a gilded coach, but in a handsome *landau* from Longacre. I remember him, after one of his cosmopolitan dinner-parties, speaking to his guests of the fine carriage horses that he had just imported from England, and insisting on the whole party coming down to the stables to inspect them. It was a picture which Rembrandt might have painted – his Eminence, in scarlet sash, stockings and cap, striding into the stalls, and regaling his favourites with big rosy apples; a bearded Armenian bishop, a dignified Protonotary Apostolic, and two domestic prelates, standing ankle-deep in the straw, holding up their violet skirts and muttering '*E proprio originale, questo cardinale inglese!*'; an amused and irreverent Oxonian (that was I!) laughing in the background; and the bright Roman sun shining from a turquoise sky on the picturesque figures, the medley of colours, and the two grinning grooms (one English, one Roman) who stood in their shirt-sleeves looking on at the quaint scene.

The Cardinal (who was above all things unconventional) never troubled himself to disguise his identity when he took the air afoot. I used sometimes to see him coming home from a visit to some church, perhaps the *stazione* of the day; and a notable figure he was, walking rapidly along (as his custom was) in his red-buttoned cassock and scarlet sash, big hat with gold and scarlet tassels, and silver-buckled shoes. A liveried lackey followed him at a respectful distance, bearing his breviary, prayer-books, and other implements of devotion; and the little Romans would gaze up at the *gran cardinale inglese* with mingled admiration and astonishment. A splendid apparition of that kind had, in truth, already become rare in the Rome of 1880; and his Eminence attracted nearly as much attention in the raw unfinished streets of *Buzurropolis* as he would have done had he taken a noonday stroll in similar costume from Charing Cross to Ludgate Circus.

I was present when Cardinal Howard received the *biglietto* announcing his elevation to the sacred purple in 1877, and also when he took possession of his titular church, SS. John and Paul, which, two centuries before, his kinsman, Cardinal Philip Howard, O.P., had acquired for the English Dominicans, and had spent large sums in restoring and beautifying.

I think that almost my last glimpse of the kind English Cardinal was seeing him in some recreation-hall in the Vatican, whither Pope Pius IX used to come down after his solitary dinner for half an hour's conversation with his cardinals. We chamberlains had the privilege of standing, mute as mice, behind the high-backed seats on which their Eminences sat in due order and talked, the Holy Father in the centre of the circle. Cardinal '*Ovardi*' (the nearest that the Romans could get to the noble name of Howard) was seated as a mere cardinal deacon, furthest away from his Holiness, who, however, I remember on one occasion called him to come and sit beside him, and tell him the news from England, especially what that dreadful '*Gladston-ey*' had lately been saying about Rome and the Pope. During this brief recreation the Pope always circulated his snuff-box (with a magnificent cameo on its lid) round the distinguished circle; and if anyone passed it on without taking a pinch – Cardinal *'Ovardi'* never did – the Pontiff would call out playfully, *'Eminenza! non prende? perche?'*

The last five years of Cardinal Howard's life were spent in England, and clouded by trying and incurable illness. But he never lost the love and respect of his devoted relatives and friends; and this was abundantly testified at the great gathering which attended his impressive funeral in 1892 in the historic Fitz-Alan Chapel at Arundel.

This article originally appeared in the April 1936 edition of 'The Venerabile'.

Alumnus Collegij Anglicani

A student of the English College in 1710. College dress remained unchanged until the 1960s.

'Dear Old Monte Porzio' – Seminarians on Vacation, 1820–1920

Nicholas Schofield

A little northeast from Frascati lies the sleepy *Castelli* town of Monte Porzio. The name may not mean a great deal to many readers, beyond a vague recollection of having read it on a wine label, but for J. R. Meagher, looking back to his student days in 1925, 'the name breathes balm and benediction; it is odorous with the perfumed memories of youth'.[1] He was by no means alone. When John Joseph Mulligan left the English College in April 1841 to take up priestly work in the Midland District, he sent a number of poems to the College's Debating Society in which he eulogizes those tranquil days on the Porzian height, which must have seemed such a contrast to the demands of the English Mission. In the final verse of his 'An Evening Melody at Porzio', based on the sound of the evening *Ave Maria* in the village, he writes:

> Ave Maria, dear words that remind me
> Of times I have passed where religion is free
> Ave Maria, dear words that e'er bind me
> To one loving spot in my lov'd Italy.[2]

The most celebrated Porzio enthusiast was Cardinal Wiseman, whose thoughts returned there as he lay on his deathbed:

> I am sure it would do me more good to have a long talk about Monte Porzio than to be kept so much alone ... I can see the colour of the chestnut trees, and Camaldoli, and the top of Tusculum. What a beautiful view it is from our Refectory window! A newcomer does not value Monte Porzio properly. It takes a hard year's work in Rome to enable you to appreciate it. I loved it dearly. I keep a picture of it in my bedroom ...[3]

Indeed, the extent of Wiseman's love for the place was such that, when his elevation to the cardinalate was announced before that of the restoration of the hierarchy in 1850 and he assumed he would have to live in Rome, he considered buying a villa at Monte Porzio. Even as Archbishop of Westminster he continued to visit Porzio, writing the bulk of his novel, *Fabiola*, during one of his visits. The little town with its simple piety and succession of summer feasts was as central as the Papal Court to Wiseman's idea of Catholicism. If one of his great achievements was assimilating English Catholicism to Ultramontane Italianate models, then Porzio had an important part to play in this, at least in the realm of the imagination. It was at Porzio that Wiseman fell in love with the *campagna* and its people, and perhaps his thoughts returned there as he visited the more rural parts of Westminster.

What attraction did this obscure town have for generations of Englishmen? It was in this *Citta del vino* that, from the early seventeenth century up until 1917, the English College took its summer vacation or *villeggiatura* away from the Latin lectures, the strict College timetable and the *mal aria* of Rome.

Monte Porzio was first used for a College *villeggiatura* in 1614. The College rented a property belonging to the

English Jesuits, which had been bought out of a bequest given for missionary purposes by the celebrated convert, Sir Tobie Mathew, son of an Archbishop of York. These moneys had also resulted in the purchase of the La Magliana vineyard, seven miles out of Rome and managed by English Jesuit lay brothers, whose revenues helped to finance the Jesuit College at Liège. The vineyard was used by the English College for free days until 1917 where students could enjoy a mealtime treat of *abacchi* hash, plum pie and wine *ad libitum*. The property at Monte Porzio, which consisted of vineyards and lands, including some at nearby Monte Compatri, was finally purchased for the College in 1708. Porzio was almost lost to the College in the mid-1870s, when new laws regarding church property in Rome required the selling of property not actually occupied by the community. However, the day was saved by a cunning plan devised by the Rector, Henry O'Callaghan, whereby the College's property was put up for auction and bought by the Duke of Norfolk, 'for and on behalf' of the College. To keep up appearances, a coronetted 'N' could supposedly be seen branded on the tubs of La Magliona: Confiscation was therefore avoided, although Porzio would be sold forty years later after a Visitation deemed the villa unhealthy and unsuitable for the needs of the College.

The old villa, to be found on the Via Verdi, is today a rather dilapidated complex comprising of a *carabinieri* station, a small shop and an excellent *trattoria* (*Cantina Romoletto*), with a very tasty *salsiccia* dish. In its external appearance, the villa cannot have changed much since that last *villeggiatura* of 1917. 'A cross between a catacomb and a rabbit warren',[4] it was basically three houses knocked into one – 'humble, uncomfortable, ramshackle, not over-clean' but 'for three months in the summer it was an English oasis in an alien wilderness'.[5] The villa, 'with its dark and rambling staircases, its brick floors, and its hundred minor discomforts ... certainly had the advantage of contrast to the stately halls and spacious corridors of the College in Rome'. All in all the Porzian experience was 'tolerated with Spartan courage for the sake of the lovely country to which it gave ready access'.[6] And, indeed, the natural location was beautiful, as can be seen in Wiseman's idyllic description:

> While the entrance and front of the villa are upon the regular streets of the little town, the garden side stands upon the verge of the hilltop and the view, after plunging at once to the depths of the valley, along which runs a shady road, rises up a gentle acclivity, vine and olive-clad, above which is clasped a belt of stately chestnuts, the bread-tree of the Italian peasant, and thence springs up a round craggy mount looking stern and defiant, like what it was – the citadel of Tusculum.[7]

The *villeggiatura* normally stretched from August to October, and there was often a holiday at Porzio at Easter. However, the villa was not merely a *casa di villeggiatura*. Students went there to recover from illness and to shelter from troubles in Rome. During the cholera epidemic of 1837, for instance, the students moved from the College, which was used as a hospital, and even established a committee of health while away. Porzio itself escaped the epidemic.[8] Students also escaped there at Pentecost 1889, when the new statue of Giordano Bruno was unveiled in the Campo de'Fiori. The Gregorian University was ordered to close for a week due to fears of radical anti-clericalism and the students could enjoy the pleasures of the *campagna* in June.[9]

The journeying between Rome and Porzio was not always one way. On 12 September 1869 William Kirkham recorded in his diary: 'At 11am was disturbed in my room by [William] Gordon coming and saying that fighting was going on in the direction of Socrates and that the fellows on Tusculum had heard the cannonading going on all morning. On going to the Parish Church only heard one shot. So it has begun!'[10] What had been heard was not fighting but the blowing up of a bridge by papal troops in preparation for the expected siege, but nonetheless it was decided that the students should return to the Via di Monserrato for safety. The spirit of the *villeggiatura* continued as the Union Flag was raised over the College entrance, students toured the city fortifications and listened eagerly for gunfire, and the community was sent into the cellar as the fighting intensified, where they were served with hot wine. They returned to Porzio on 30 September. Other dramatic events could also disturb the rhythms of the Porzian summer, such as a conclave. On 4 August 1903 Pius X was elected pope, and H. E. Hazlehurst recorded 'great commotion' in his diary – 'worked all afternoon getting out illuminations, etc. Designed a *Pio X*. We had a grand show; band came, the whole village turned out; a balloon, etc'. Having already travelled into Rome to pay their respects to Leo XIII a fortnight before – 'the face is quite changed and discoloured: not nice' – the students caught the train on 9 August for the Coronation. Hazlehurst had a 'grand view of Pope' although 'he looked quite upset: tears in his eyes, made no movement'.[11]

What was the *villeggiatura* itself like at Monte Porzio? Everyday student life remains peculiarly elusive to the historian, at least up until the time of Mgr Giles and the advent of *The Venerabile* in 1922. The student diaries we have in the Archive tend to concentrate on details of churches visited, papal liturgies attended and dignitaries spoken to, rather than personal details of what to them, perhaps, seemed mundane and normal, but what to us would contain much interest. Even personal milestones such as Ordination Day were reported in a handful of lines and in a matter-of-fact way. However, we are fortunate when it comes to the topic of Porzio, for the diaries contain often quite detailed descriptions of their recreations, excursions and *feste*. To reconstruct those sweltering months at Porzio, we will largely draw upon student diaries and memoirs stretching from the 1820s up until the last days of Rector Giles. Although these cover different regimes and generations, the basic 'Porzian experience' remained more or less the same. By ploughing through such sources, we begin to feel very much 'in touch' with these long-dead seminarists, seeing them not so much as names in the *Liber Ruber* but as young men in search of rest and recreation after long months of formal study.

The summer timetable showed more flexibility than that in Rome. It usually began with meditation and Mass in the small chapel on the top floor of the house, which was 'nearly always 60° before we crowded in'.[12] Nor was the intense heat the only obstacle to prayer, for it was 'very hard to keep one's eyes from wandering to the windows through which, on the one side, the rising sun may be seen approaching over the house-tops, and on the other, the open *campagna* stretching towards Rome'.[13] After breakfast, students were supposed to go to their rooms until eleven, 'doing something useful', as the rules put it. Indeed, 'the new men used to be frightened in advance, being told that even in holidays they had to study all the morning, but no one could move, even in the shade, until the sea breeze waved the acacias punctually at eleven'.[14] How much study was actually accomplished in the heat of the villa is uncertain – in August 1853 the Rector, Robert Cornthwaite, spoke to the students about 'reading novels in time which ought to be given to *bona fide* study'.[15] After midday the students climbed up to the cramped chapel for Rosary and Prayers for England, and returned there for a 'Visit' after lunch. Recreation followed – during which one could read, gather round the piano or play cards, chess or billiards on a table which 'like the villa, bears the mark of antiquity'. Gradually the common room emptied as the sacred siesta approached – a time when, we are assured, 'the whole village is wrapped in the deepest slumber'.[16] Another student recalled that 'you could hear the village breathing deeply, and the thousand million flies drying up sliced tomatoes on the wooden trays on window-sills in the sun. It was all so quiet that the sounds went to decorate the silence'.[17]

A bell rudely interrupted this blissful stupor and announced tea, after which many chose to go for an evening stroll, perhaps to Tusculum or the nearby Camaldolese monastery, which had been a favourite haunt of the 'Old Pretender'. Tusculum played an important role in the months at Porzio. Rich in natural beauty and historical associations – it was on the site of a Roman town and the stronghold of the medieval Dukes of Tusculum, until it was razed by Celestine III in 1191 – it was easily accessible from the villa grounds. Sometime in the mid-nineteenth century members of the College erected a wooden cross on the summit, the progenitor of the present steel cross, which was placed there in 1934. In 1891 the third Tusculum cross was found desecrated – sawn off at the base and with a Masonic message attached – although the holidaying students quickly raised a new cross to the loud singing of *Pange Lingua*, 'Faith of Our Fathers' and *O Roma Felix*.[18] On the summit of Tusculum, students rambled and dozed in the shade, wrote poetry, held breakfasts and dinners, hunted for skulls and other ancient relics or even caught butterflies. This latter activity seemed particularly popular. On 10 August 1853, George Johnson recorded that he had been 'out catching butterflies nearly all day' and several weeks later he was looking for 'emperor caterpillars, nearly giving up in despair when we found a beautiful one'. On one occasion he rather daringly 'got a good moth from [the] rector's rooms'.[19] He could also be found hunting and killing vipers, or 'setting lime twigs to catch my old feathered friends'. On 22 February 1854, whilst recuperating from a serious illness, he caught a goldfinch and a wren in such a trap.[20] For those who remained at the villa, there was also – under Giles – the option of tennis in the orchard.

At eight, dinner was served in the refectory. Before Night Prayers closed the day, students would typically gather on the terrace where, 'in easy chairs, the walkers rest their tired limbs, and drink in the delights of the cool Italian night'. Discussion could be lively; 'a balcony argument', wrote A. N. Barrie, a member of the last generation to use Monte Porzio, 'has come to mean one which is carried on *ad infinitum*'.[21] There might be other evening pastimes. One evening in 1829 there was 'a French juggler in ye College who performed very well in cards, changing sums of money, with his dancing harlequin'.[22] Under Cornthwaite, students might repair to the common room to read *The Porzio Post*, a student rag, which anticipated the more famous *Chi Lo Sa?* of the twentieth century.[23]

The highlight of the week was the daylong excursions in the surrounding countryside. These would often include a picnic lunch and an open-air *siesta*. 'If anyone happened to come upon this scene,' speculated one student, 'he could not but think that a massacre of the clergy had taken place, for he would find the ground strewn with the bodies of clerical students in the most contorted attitudes.'[24] However, certain rules had to be followed. On the first day of the 1903 *villeggiatura*, for example, the students were told that bathing was only allowed after the Tusculum dinner. Moreover, 'speaking of going in *osteria*'s etc on long walks, [the staff] knew there was one at Rocca di Papa much frequented so that the women went by a familiar name: That house is forbidden, out of bounds'.[25]

Palazzola was a popular destination – on 25 October 1853, Johnson recorded in his diary that he 'dined in the convent there, a most beautiful place and affording some magnificent views'.[26] George Ambrose Burton went there with Mgr Giles in September 1888 – 'we dined in the Refectory of Capuchins, into which a tribe of coenobitical cats every now and then furtively intruded, to be whipped out with little ceremony by a snow bearded friar, who, having spent some years in the neighbourhood of the Tigris, delighted to regale us with morsels of Arabic'.[27] He was there again the following year – 'here I visited the Church and garden again, and then went up to dine in the faded *saloon* upstairs. After grace I went down the wooded declivity below ... and sat for a good while in the sun'.[28]

Many students got to know the villagers during their

three-month stay at Porzio, although they often displayed a rather patronizing and chauvinistic approach to the local population. Richard Browne's diary shows a particular interest in socio-economic information. Writing about a young vintner he met in September 1829, Browne records his hours of work, wages, diet and educational details, and concludes his observations in the manner of a parliamentary commissioner: 'I take this boy for a fair specimen of ye fixed or resident village labouring class'.[29] On meeting 'a sick youth' several weeks later, he notes that many Porzians 'would rather die at home in misery than go to the hospital [in Rome], for they thought they would be expedited there quickly either being killed or turned out', and that they called the hospital the *anticamera della casa del diavolo*.[30] That same summer Browne interviewed 'a civil husbandman' and 'a charcoal carrier with 4 sacks on an ass'.[31]

The *villeggiatura* coincided with the main village feasts. On these occasions the students joined the local community for Mass in the parish church, where the organ was reported to have 'resembled a broken pair of bagpipes'.[32] 2 September saw the festa of the village patron, St Antoninus, and the *'Nobile Collegio Inglese'* would assist at Mass and the procession of the relic, as well as listen to the village band and watch the fireworks and balloons. On 24 September it was the feast of the village's patroness, St Laconella, an early virgin martyr whose bones, coated in *paper mache*, were in the parish church. There were also red-letter days for the villa: St Edward, the villa's patron, on 13 October and, more importantly, the feast of Our Lady of Good Hope on 8 September, whose miraculous image was proudly housed in a shrine attached to the villa. Mass was said at the shrine, which was decorated with lights. The villa itself was covered with Chinese lanterns, lamps, *transparenze* and garlands spelling *Ave Maria*.

The visit of important guests was another treat for the students. On 7 October 1847, for instance, the newly ordained John Henry Newman dined there with Dr Grant and Dr Sharples, having walked in the morning towards Monte Cavo.[33] No records exist of what the students thought of their famous guest. When Cardinal Wiseman arrived at his beloved Monte Porzio for a day in October 1853, the students 'gave him as good a cheer as 21 voices could as he drove up'. During dinner 'the [village] band played for him in their uniforms' and over *caffe e rosolio*, he told the assembled company 'a great many anecdotes about the old college'.[34]

Two popes visited the villa during the nineteenth century: Leo XII on 29 October 1827 and Blessed Pius IX on 5 September 1864, both commemorated by slabs which were translated to the refectory at Palazzola in 1920. The visit of Leo XII has been particularly well described. In late September 1827 the sluggish *villeggiatura* was suddenly interrupted by a profusion of activity. College hangings and furniture arrived, together with a fine fatted calf from the Borghese farm of Pantano. In the village itself, roads were repaired, streets cleaned, tapestries hung out and triumphal arches built. On the morning of the great day, students could be seen leaning over the garden wall, carefully watching the road from Frascati along which the pontifical entourage was expected to appear at any moment. At last, a glint of a dragoon helmet and sword was spotted, followed by the papal carriage itself, which before long was parked outside the villa. Pope Leo walked to the parish church to pray, before going to a house in the main square where he met the important Porzians and blessed the villagers from a balcony. He then went to the English villa for lunch, where he spoke to all and commented: 'it is seldom that a poor Pope can enjoy the pleasure of sitting down to dinner with such a fine set of men'. After taking a *siesta* in the Rector's room, he met the local clergy, 'able though plain, and certainly most disinterested men', sitting in a rush chair and not in the throne prepared for him. The Pontiff obviously enjoyed his visit, presenting the College the following Easter with a 'fine, fat, live calf with a halter of red silk and gold on its head, its feet tied with red silk cords to the litter, and its head and neck adorned with beautiful garlands of artificial fruits and flowers' – a treat enjoyed by all the English Catholics in Rome.[35]

Life continued at Porzio into the first years of the twentieth century. If the figure of Mgr Giles became so synonymous with the College during his long Rectorship (1888–1913) that it was known as *Palazzo Giles* then surely the summerhouse at Porzio became the *Villa Giles*. His rooms there effectively became a painting and photographic studio during the *villeggiatura*, and his many fine watercolours of the area remain one of the most vivid monuments to Porzio in the present College, as are the famous photos of his breakfasts on Tusculum. The student's fondness for 'the Gi' is captured in the celebrations for his Golden Jubilee of Priesthood in August 1904. The house was decorated and a 'canopy of ivy leaves and gold braid with *ad multos annos* in leaves on red background' was erected in the refectory. Even the village band offered to play, but Giles, perhaps on account of his refined musical tastes, declined the kind offer. A paper balloon was also constructed with a picture of a precious and plain mitre with the words *Tu es Sacerdos in aeternum*. Unfortunately it collapsed as it was being hoisted and 'part of it blew into a neighbouring tree'.[36]

With Giles' death in 1913 a chapter in College history closed. Things were changing as war clouds loomed. The visitation completed in 1916 resulted in the recommendation that Porzio should be sold since it was unsuitable and unhealthy especially given student numbers. The last *villeggiatura* was spent there in 1917, and the then rector, Arthur Hinsley, began looking for a new villa. Meanwhile, a community of Elizabettine nuns, fleeing from the fighting in north Italy, moved into the Porzio house. Hinsley eventually persuaded them to move into the College to look after the domestic arrangements – in which capacity they remained until 1995.[37]

The summer of 1918 was spent at a former friary at

Montopoli in Sabina, with an adjoining church boasting 'gaudily decorated pillars and trumpeting angels'. When news of the Armistice arrived, Hinsley declared a 'no bell day' and presided at a solemn Benediction and *Te Deum*. The previous evening a crowd of *Montopoliani* had approached the villa shouting *Evviva l'Inghilterra!*[38] The stay was extended by the Spanish flu that was meanwhile wiping out the inmates of Amaldi's recently established health camp at Palazzola. This former Capuchin convent had already captured Hinsley's attention, and negotiations were begun with the proprietor. Hinsley managed to snap it up for an amazingly low price – everything was included, even the cutlery, which fortuitously bore the initials 'C. A.', interchangeably 'Carlo Amaldi' and '*Collegium Anglorum*'.

In the heart of the Alban hills, there are many continuities between Palazzola and Porzio – not least of which are the slabs in the refectory commemorating papal visits to the old villa or the venerable tradition of Mass on Tusculum during the *villeggiatura*, even if it is four times further away now. Palazzola is undoubtedly a finer place in almost every aspect – location, architecture, and history. J. R. Meagher admitted that 'no one regrets the change', but still found that memories of 'the taste of wine, the smell of garlic, the sound of a bell, the drowsy peace of a summer's night [could] play havoc with emotions and call up the gentle ghosts of exultant days'. For 'as a roof and walls, Monte Porzio meant little to us; but as the gateway to Romance, the very thought of it thrilled us'.[39] Generations of students – going back to the reign of James I and almost certainly including some of 'the Forty-Four' – had rested, studied, played and been formed at 'dear old Monte Porzio', almost all had fallen in love with 'this lovely spot' and many had found God in the stuffy chapel or the rolling woods.[40] The unassuming little village has thus has a subtle and unique place in English Catholic history and has summed up for many what the 'Roman experience' was all about. Its important place in the consciousness of many English priests down the ages is expressed by Mulligan's 'Farewell to Porzio', on which note we too shall end:

> Once more, loved spot – farewell, farewell!
> Sweet Porzio dear, a long adieu!
> You've won my heart, you've bound a spell
> Around my soul of love for you! –
> One only wish with thee I leave, –
> May every neighbouring grove and dell
> Long echo back my heart's fond heave
> To each and all – farewell! farewell![41]

Note on the Sources

The following sources were consulted from VEC Archives:
Liber 588 – Register Book for College Debating Society, 1841 (inc. poems by Rev. John Joseph Mulligan, VEC 1833–41)
Liber 821 – Diary of George Johnson 1852–3 (VEC 1852–3)
Liber 824 – Diary of George Burton 1884–90 (VEC 1884–90)
Liber 828 – Reminiscences of Canon Richard Burke (VEC 1898–1905, copied 1933)
Liber 829 – Diary of Henry Hazlehurst 1901–5 (VEC 1898–1905)
Scr.80.11 Diary of William Kirkham 1869–73 (VEC 1869–73)
Scr.122.1 Diary of Richard Browne 1825–30 (VEC 1825–30)

Notes

1. J. R. Meagher, 'Monte Porzio' in *The Venerabile*, vol. II (October 1925), 211.
2. Liber 588.
3. W. Ward, *The Life and Times of Cardinal Wiseman*, vol. 2, 1898, pp. 510–11.
4. J. O'Connor, 'Monte Porzio Catone' in *The Venerabile*, vol. x (November 1941), 119.
5. Meagher, op. cit.
6. Anon., 'Nova et vetera' in *The Venerabile*, vol. III (October 1927), 262.

7. N. Wiseman, *Recollections of the Last Four Popes and of Rome in their Times*, 1858, pp. 185–6.
8. M. Williams, *The Venerable English College Rome*, 1979, p. 98.
9. A. Moriarty, 'The Late Eighties' in *The Venerabile*, vol. XII (May 1945), 123.
10. VEC Archive *Scritture (Scr.)* 80. 11 – entry for 12 September 1869.
11. VEC Archive *Liber* 829 – entries for 24 July, 4 and 9 August 1903.
12. O'Connor, op. cit., 120.
13. Barrie, 'Summer Vacation in the Alban Hills' in *Baeda*, vol. 3 (December 1917), 147.
14. O'Connor, op. cit.
15. VEC Archive Liber 821 – entry for 27 August 1853.
16. Barrie, op. cit.
17. O'Connor, op. cit.
18. K. Haggerty, 'The English College and Tusculum: The Unfolding of Tradition' in *The Venerabile*, vol. XXIX, no. 4, 29–44 (1990).
19. VEC Archive Liber 821 – entries for 10, 26 and 31 August 1853.
20. Ibid. – entries for 19 March and 22 February 1854.
21. Barrie, op. cit., 150.
22. VEC Archive *Scr.* 122. 1. 2 – entry for 15 September 1829.
23. Anon., 'College Rectors V: Robert Cornthwaite' in *The Venerabile*, vol. IV (April 1930), 361.
24. Barrie, op. cit., 151.
25. VEC Archive Liber 829 – entry for 17 July 1903.
26. VEC Archive Liber 821 – entry for 25 October 1853.
27. VEC Archive Liber 824 – entry for 20 September 1888.
28. Ibid. – entry for 9 October 1889.
29. VEC Archive *Scr.* 122. 1. 2 – entry for 7 September 1829.
30. Ibid. – entry for 13 October 1829.
31. Ibid. – entry for 21 October 1829.
32. VEC Archive Liber 821 – entry for 31 August 1853.
33. *LDXII*, 124.
34. VEC Archive Liber 821 – entry for 27 October 1853.
35. Wiseman, op. cit., 313–22.
36. VEC Archive Liber 828 – entries for 24 and 25 August 1904.
37. Williams, op. cit., 150–6.

38. J. Scarr & R. Meagher, 'Montopoli' in *The Venerabile*, vol. VI (October 1933), 277–93.
39. Meagher, op. cit., 212–3.
40. VEC Archive Liber 824 – entry for 24 July 1890: 'Said the Community Mass in our little chapel at the top of the house wherein I have received so many graces from God'. The following day Burton wrote: 'Enjoyed my last afternoon sprawl under the acacias of the *Pio* garden: breeze was fresher than ever, skies bluer, the hills green.'
41. VEC Archive Liber 588.

This article first appeared in the 2001 edition of 'The Venerabile'.

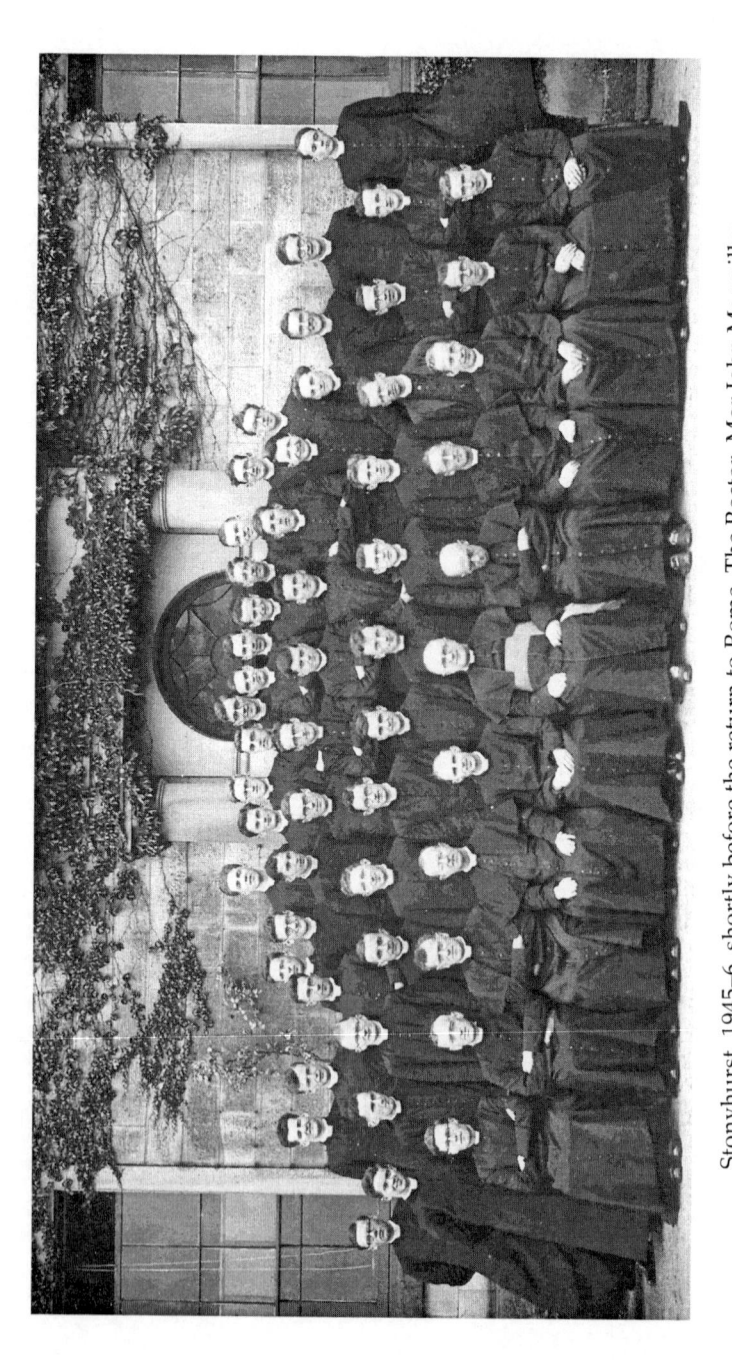

Stonyhurst, 1945–6, shortly before the return to Rome. The Rector, Mgr John Macmillan, is seated at the centre of the front row. The author, Richard Stewart, can be seen on the back row, fifth from the left.

'That English Romayne Life': Exile at Stonyhurst (1940–46)

Richard L. Stewart

On 15 May 1940 the English College was evacuated for the first time since 1798. The exiled community managed to catch the last boat out of Le Havre before the port fell and collegiate life continued more or less as normal first at Croft Lodge, Ambleside, and then at Stonyhurst. Here Richard Stewart, at the time a fresh-faced student for Southwark, looks back to those distant days of exile – a peculiarly English 'Romayne life'.

Any commemoration of the English College, Rome would be incomplete – at least for those who studied there – without some reference to St Mary's Hall, Stonyhurst. This austere building ensured the continuity of the College over a difficult six years (1940–46). The efforts of the Rector, Mgr Macmillan, and of the two Vice-Rectors, Mgr Smith and Fr Grasar, with the solid backing of the Apostolic Delegate, Archbishop Godfrey, himself a former Rector, were vital to the preservation of the community that is the College.

Writing many years later, it is perilously easy, especially for those who never knew 'the Hall', to smile gently at the *Romanità*, even the romanticism of those days. To live an English Roman life was by no means easy, for Lancashire is hardly Lazio. A diligent reader of the 1940–46 issue of *The Venerabile*, particularly of the College Diaries, may find it all sounds a little bit precious. Can men really go on *gita* to Blackpool, or even to Ribchester? Wasn't it distinctly odd to have an annual catacombs mass in the little Catholic Church next to the ruins of Whalley Abbey? And how pathetic to discover that on *feste* in those days there was still coffee and 'liqs' (though a resolute apologete might argue that the small glasses of undiluted lime juice at least looked like *Strega*).[1] All in all, the reader of today may be tempted to dismiss the whole thing as hopelessly artificial. Not that men of the time were unaware of this: one *Chi Lo Sa?*[2] contained a telling sketch of the war memorial at Burst Green, the nearest conurbation, with the simple caption 'de Urbe'.

Yet the preservation in an English setting of traditional ways and phraseology drawn from elsewhere is not a phenomenon exclusively reserved to this Venerable English College. To take just one example: we were living in the grounds of Stonyhurst College, which had left the continent some 150 years earlier but still kept (and keeps) its 'Blandyke Days' named after a spot near St Omers.[3]

As students do, we took many things for granted. But looking back one begins to appreciate what a heavy burden the superiors of that time had to bear. To leave Rome at short notice in May, to find temporary accommodation in Ambleside almost immediately, and to open the College as a going concern in a suitable building in time for the Autumn Term would be a remarkable feat at any time, *a fortiori* in post-Dunkirk England (the summer of the Battle of Britain and of serious expectation of invasion). After all, it was not just a matter of finding a building. Buildings need furniture; in the event much of this came from a recently defunct seminary at Leeds – and, clearly, it had been well used. A college needs a library: quite a reasonable one was built up, largely through the generosity of other colleges, old students and a host of benefactors. There was need for nuns to man the kitchen, if that is the right phrase; the Sisters of Saint Joseph of Peace of Newark rallied round. Local tradesmen had to be convinced that there were worthwhile customers here in those days of rationing. Bishops had to be reassured that the College was viable and that it was still worthwhile sending students there. And, since there was no Gregorian University in Lancashire, a teaching staff had to be gathered there.

The philosophical flag was kept flying throughout these years by Fr George Ekberry, who was already the *ripetitore*; Moral Theology was seen to by Dr Butterworth. The Rector and Vice did their bit with various courses (including Italian lessons for the First Year). We started with the sentence *'Andiamo alla sacra Congregazione per i seminari e l'Universitil degli Studi'*, a sentence I have never used in real life. For much else we owed teaching to the generosity of the English Jesuits, who would come up to the Hall to teach the theological courses they had been giving to their own students at Heythrop; and it was through Heythrop that our theologians were able to get genuine Greg licentiates. It would be invidious to single out names, but no one will forget Fr Bob Dyson who for much of this period lived in the College as Prefect of Studies. As students, I repeat, we took so much of this for granted: but as time passes it is easier to recognize the difficult transfer willingly taken on by two priests, both former students, who came to help the College during its last year or so in England. Dr Tom Lynch came, within weeks of his release from a prisoner of war camp, to teach history of philosophy; and immediately on demobilization, Dr Patsy Redmond, who, as army chaplain had 'taken possession' of the College on the very day Rome was liberated in 1944, was lecturing to us on metaphysics, still for the first week or two in his khaki battledress.

In other words, beneath any apparent 'romanticism', the real work of the place, the training and formation of priests, was carrying on, in a realistic way at no small cost to those responsible. It was not an easy time. Men whose families lived in frequently bombed areas, or whose fathers and brothers were in the armed forces, had their unsettling worries and sometimes their bereavements. Men who were torn between a sense of vocation and a feeling that they ought to be with their contemporaries in the forces cannot always have been easy to counsel. And, of course, original sin continued to have its effects: as in any college at any time and in any place, there were the usual domestic upheavals and 'stirs'.

Here it was that, whatever its apparent artificiality, our English Roman life had its part to play. These were years in which, more than at any other time, the College needed that elusive and indefinable thing, its 'spirit'. Like the patriotism of the time, it may have taken some odd forms, but it did the trick – but only just. The final year in England was a difficult one: by then Rome was becoming not so much a memory as an abstract ideal, something a little removed from time and place (as old College song books amply demonstrate). Then suddenly it began to become real again. It is a tribute to those who organized the English Roman life that in October 1946 those of us who had been some years in the College but had never yet seen Rome really did feel, as our taxis deposited us in the Via di Monserrato for the first time, that we were 'coming back'.

Notes

1. It was customary to have 'liqs' (liqueurs) after meals on great feasts. By the 1940s, *Strega* seems to have replaced *rosolio* as the most popular College 'liq'.
2. *Chi Lo Sa?* was a collection of satirical writings and cartoons produced by students several times a year for distribution within the house. This was produced up until the 1960s.
3. 'Blandyke' is named after Blandecques Abbey, a Cistercian foundation near Saint-Omers.

These memories of Stonyhurst were first recorded in 'The Venerabile' for 1979, which celebrated the Fourth Centenary of the College.

Students at St Peter's in October 1946, including the author on the right of the photograph.

Cardinal George Basil Hume, O.S.B.

Basil Hume Remembered

Gerard Skinner

> I trusted, even when I said:
> 'I am sorely afflicted,'
> and when I said in my alarm:
> 'No man can be trusted.'
> (Ps. 116:10–11)

Learning of the gravity of his illness, Cardinal George Basil Hume, O.S.B., went straight to the hospital chapel and prayed. The dawn so longed for by all monks was fast approaching. Writing to his brother priests in his Archdiocese, he spoke of the two graces that he had received: time to prepare himself for death, and the gift of peace.

For a while, he continued to fulfil as many engagements as possible, but soon, sooner than expected, the cancer took hold. Sitting in his study in Archbishop's House, he called a passing priest to come in. The Cardinal said that he could no longer pray; all he could do was look at the crucifix. This form of prayer he had often spoken about in healthier days – when words fail, just look upon the cross, just kiss that cross. His last public engagement was to receive the Order of Merit from Her Majesty the Queen at Buckingham Palace, an engagement he had ardently wished to fulfil. Even though permanently confined to hospital, he left for the Palace from Archbishop's House, and returned there afterwards to celebrate and bid farewell to his staff. During these days of his suffering, there occurred so many moments of humour and kindness, which could only be expressed by one who trusted in his Lord. At 5.20 p.m. on Thursday 17 June, fortified by the love and prayers of the Church, he passed away. How quickly he went.

> How can I repay the Lord
> For his goodness to me?
> The cup of salvation I will raise;
> I will call on the Lord's name.
> (Ps. 116:12–13)

George Hume – he took the name Basil when he was clothed with the habit – was born on 2 March 1923 in Newcastle-upon-Tyne, the son of Sir William Errington Hume, C.M.G., F.R.C.P., a distinguished physician, and Marie Elisabeth, his devout French wife. The children were raised bilingually.

George was aware of his Benedictine calling from the age of eleven, when he was enrolled as a pupil at Ampleforth College; he entered the monastery immediately upon leaving the school in 1941. Years later, talking with his seminarians, he would recall how, during the long hours of prayer and meditation, he would sit in the Abbey Church, bored stiff. Yet, looking across at his fellow novices, they seemed to be so angelic in their countenances that they must have been in deep prayer. It was some time before he had the courage to ask them the secret, admitting that his prayer life did not seem so rich. Sadly, whatever they might have looked like, they were suffering in much the same way. To his students, the Cardinal always advocated fixed times of community meditation – the need to sit there, whether easy or hard. It certainly became very hard for him, and, one time, he approached a wise old monk telling him of his intention to leave the monastery. The monk listened and discussed his problems, finally making the novice promise that he would not leave until he (the old monk) returned from hospital from what was expected to be a relatively minor operation. The old monk died – and so Dom Basil remained!

During his studies at St Benet's Hall, Oxford (1944–1947), Dom Basil took Solemn Vows in 1945. He completed his studies with a licentiate in theology from the University of Freibourg in Switzerland (1951). He was ordained priest at Ampleforth on 23 July 1950. The life of a monk is popularly misconstrued as one of total peace and tranquility – lines of hooded black-cowled monks holding candles in a nocturnal procession with sonorous abbey bells and profound murmured chants. By way of contrast, Dom Basil was hurled into the life of the Abbey and College, a life which is indeed busy. For a while, he was assistant priest at Ampleforth village, whilst teaching at the school. Then, he became housemaster of one of the boarding houses, and head of modern languages. He taught the monks dogmatic theology, and was elected *Magister Scholorum* of the English Benedictine Congregation by their 1957 General Chapter. Later, he would say that these were some of the happiest years of his life: he was responsible yet free, and not weighed down with office – too good, he thought, to last.

> My vows to the Lord I will fulfil
> Before all his people.
> (Ps. 116:14)

In 1963, Dom Basil was elected Abbot of Ampleforth. He succeeded Abbot Byrne, a monk of great age who had been Abbot for many years, and whom Dom Basil greatly respected. Forty is a young age to be elected Abbot – in total, the late Cardinal served for thirty-six years as a major superior or bishop. The times were also seemingly inauspicious. The very first document to come out of the Second Vatican Council (1962–1965), the Constitution on the Sacred Liturgy, *Sacrosanctum Concilium* (4 December

1963), cut through to the heart of the monks' daily life, the praise of God in the liturgy. Soon, the manner of formation and the monastic life itself were to be the subjects of reform. As every seminarian knows, that which should so deeply unite is often where the Devil is so quick to cause division. In later years, the Cardinal reflected on such problems:

> How can you be a bishop in such situations without falling between stools or sitting on the fence? I experienced division when I was an abbot. I decided that what united people has to be very deep. It is the life of prayer. Get that right and much else falls into place.

The unity of the monastery was to be a strong signal to Archbishop Bruno Heim, the Apostolic Delegate, when he was looking for a helmsman to succeed Cardinal John Carmel Heenan in steering the Church in England and Wales away from the potentially perilous rocks of extremism that lay hidden in the choppy waters of European Catholicism in the wake of the Council. Ampleforth Abbey is a testimony to Abbot Hume's wise leadership. The community is thriving and no age range is unrepresented. Wisdom seems to percolate down through the generations of monks, from eldest to youngest, in what is an ideal and natural model for formation. In prayer, it seems that Abbot Hume discerned with his monks the way ahead, conserving and renewing, not clinging to traditions simply because they were monastic, but exalting those which were thought to be good. The image of the Abbot, like that of the monk, is largely and popularly one of the contemplative. At the heart of the matter, this must be true. But from contemplation Abbot Hume was to guide over 150 monks in his community. There was the school, twenty far-flung parishes, a daughter house in St Louis, USA, and, of course, all the mundane but necessary issues that would be discussed in Council and Chapter meetings, such as fundraising, planning, building, the farm, and so on. His preparation for Westminster – indeed, his life in Westminster – was far more practical than usually suspected. Nevertheless, administration was not his main task. Dom Dominic Milroy, a monk of Ampleforth, has described what the Rule of St Benedict asks of the Abbot:

> St Benedict requires him to be, not a chief executive, but a loving father of the community; not the manager of a production line, but a discerning guide, who treats each monk 'in the way which may seem best in each case' (Ch. 64), and who takes special care of those who are most vulnerable – the elderly, the sick, the young, the troubled in spirit. Here lies the greatest challenge to the Abbot: the complete network of human relationships of which he is the focus, and which will make relentless demands on his time, his patience and his good humour.[1]

In abiding by these essential words of the Rule, Abbot Hume fulfilled his monastic vows and came to Westminster witnessing to the wonderful model of Christian leadership offered by St Benedict:

> Your servant, Lord, your servant am I;
> You have loosened my bonds.
> A thanksgiving sacrifice I make:
> I will call on the Lord's name.
> (Ps. 116:16–17)

Like so many ecclesiastical legends, there are many versions of the story concerning Abbot Hume's appointment as Archbishop of Westminster in 1976. In the last months of his life, Cardinal Heenan had invited all to consult with the Apostolic Delegate over who should be his successor. Among over ninety names proffered, the name of the Abbot of Ampleforth emerged as a promising possibility. So, Heim sent his secretary to Ampleforth on retreat to investigate. The soundings were good and while

Hume was attending a conference of abbots near Windsor, he was summoned by Heim to be consulted as to whom he thought should be the next Archbishop of Westminster. Flattered but oblivious to any danger of being asked himself, he proffered his opinion. However, in the same meeting, he was asked by the Apostolic Delegate if he would accept an offer from the Holy Father to fulfil a particular mission. The obedient monk replied 'yes', suspecting that possibly he was to be asked to become an Auxiliary Bishop somewhere. Meanwhile, as part of the consultation process, even though unofficial, *The Times* ran an article mentioning a number of names – including Abbot Hume. The Abbot was in America at the time; on returning to the United Kingdom, he saw the article, felt flattered (and is it not an expression of his humility that he could say when he was flattered?) and telephoned his mother, who laughed. Feeling a little humbled and confident that he was safe, life continued as normal until he was asked straight.

Upon the announcement of his appointment in February 1976, the Archbishop-Elect travelled down to London to familiarize himself with the people whom he was to serve. He introduced himself to Mr Murphy at the door of Archbishop's house and asked to be shown around. He spoke of the spirit of prayer imbued in the place by the late Cardinal Heenan. Despite having been used to many practical problems, he had to ask what the initials 'H.E.' stood for in the internal telephone directory. By late May 1976, he would know.

From the rolling hills of Ampleforth to the streets of Victoria, from a community of over 150 to a massive Archdiocese with over 400 secular priests, let alone the hundreds of religious sisters, brothers and priests – no wonder he nearly wept as he passed his brother monks, processing into his Mass of Ordination in Westminster Cathedral on 25 March 1976, the Solemnity of the Annunciation of the Lord. However, the homily he preached, declaring his service to the Lord and his people, flowed naturally from one who for thirteen years had been fatherly guide:

> A great bishop of the fourth century had an uncanny knack of saying important things aptly and briefly. In one of his sermons, St Augustine said of himself: *Vobis sum episcopus, vobiscum christianus.* 'I am a bishop for you, I am a Christian like you.'

As those listening were to discover, the 'uncanny knack' of Augustine was also that of Archbishop Hume.

Paul VI had settled the troubled mind of his latest Archbishop, and it was he who, two months later, created him the Cardinal Priest of San Silvestro in Capite, on 24 May 1976. In this capacity, Cardinal Hume participated in the two conclaves of 1978. In 1979, he became President of the Bishops' Conference of England and Wales, an office he was to hold until his death. In the international field, he was President of the Council of European Bishops' Conferences from 1978 until 1987, and was Relator for the Synod of Bishops on Consecrated Life in 1994, during which he resided at the English College for almost a month.

He was a frequent visitor to Rome. He did not care for long absences from his Diocese, but would travel when required and seemed to feel very much at home among the English and Welsh seminarians. He used to say that he always had an empathy for the loser, a liking for the rogue: 'A rogue is rarely conceited.' In the easy company of good-humoured students, he may have tasted a little of the rogue's recipe. Perhaps it reminded him of the boarding house and the monastery. His presence among us was always looked forward to. He would chat with the lads, serve at table, give retreats, sit down and watch the football, show that to be a man of prayer was important, and fun. Sometimes, his visits were known in advance; at other times, particularly while negotiating with the Holy See with regard to the special arrangements for former Anglican clergymen, they would be unexpected and frequent.

The National Pastoral Congress (1980) in Liverpool was one of the supreme examples of a father listening to what the family had to say, and attempting to speak with Rome about this in a language that both might understand. This was particularly important when relating the teaching of Peter to his communities in England and Wales. Particularly after the press conference in which he presented John Paul II's Encyclical Letter *Evangelium Vitae* (25 March 1995), it was good to note that even the most hardened editors and journalists had to comment that, without mitigating anything which had to be said, the Cardinal spoke to us in love and truth, in a manner attuned to the British ear.

The happiest highlight of his ministry must surely have been the first visit of a reigning Pope to Great Britain in 1982. Deftly the Cardinal had to move to ensure the success of the visit, which came shortly after the conflict in the Falkland Islands. The visit of John Paul II was a marvellous festival of faith, centred on the seven sacraments. Other highlights of his time as Archbishop of Westminster included the centenary of the laying of the foundation stone of his Cathedral. Much happened during that year of celebration: the Cathedral Choir – which he saved – gave concerts; decoration of the interior recommenced; six European cardinals gave Lenten reflections. But perhaps most wonderful of all were the 'Area Days', when each of the five Pastoral Areas of the Archdiocese came to the Cathedral to celebrate together. Nothing was more apparent than the love in which the people held their Bishop, and the love that he had for them. He held them in his prayers, calling on the Lord's name. This love was to express itself again as the pilgrim Cardinal prepared to be taken by the Lord.

> My vows to the Lord I will fulfil
> Before all his people,
> In the courts of the house of the Lord,
> In your midst, O Jerusalem.
>
> (Ps. 116:16–17)

Some years ago, the Administrator of Westminster Cathedral approached the sculptor, Elizabeth Frink, about commissioning her to create two bronze sculptures for the Cathedral, one of St Vincent de Paul, and the other of St Benedict. Both saints have inspired many within the Cathedral's family: a very active S.V.P. group bears testimony to the former, and the witness of our beloved Father in Christ, Cardinal Hume, spoke eloquently of the latter. Sadly, Frink was to die shortly after receiving her commission and the project went into abeyance.

Two years later, however, the project sprang to life again, and in September 1998 a fine bronze of St Vincent de Paul by Bryan Kneale was unveiled. A few months earlier, the Cardinal had been approached with regard to fundraising among the Benedictine schools for the bronze of St Benedict. 'I thought that that would be a memorial to me!' he quipped before giving the go-ahead. But, before the sculptor could proceed, he asked the Cardinal's advice on how St Benedict should be represented. The Cardinal told him the story of a vision St Benedict had towards the close of his earthly life. The Saint had been looking out of his window when he saw what first appeared to be a great shaft of light proceeding from heaven and drawing the whole world into its beam – the *reditus* of redeemed humanity. The Cardinal did not mention that, according to St Gregory the Great, he then saw the soul of the holy Bishop of Capua, Germanus, ascending to heaven; the next morning, it was verified that Germanus had indeed passed away during the previous night. So, the Cardinal said, the Saint must be looking up. And so it has come to pass – the bronze of St Benedict looking to the heavens was ready to be unveiled as the Cardinal died.

In his dying, the Cardinal fulfilled his vows to the Lord, uniting his suffering with that of the Holy Father to the saving sacrifice of Our Lord on his cross. Speaking of the late Fr Anthony O'Sullivan,[2] he said that in living he taught us to live, and that in dying he taught us how to die. This teaching, this witness, was brought to the nation and many beyond our shores by the Cardinal's trust in the Lord during his final days. His body now lies in the Chapel of St Gregory and St Augustine in his Cathedral Church. These two saints look down upon him, along with St Cuthbert, St Bede the Venerable, St Paulinus, and many other monk-bishops of the North of England, so dearly loved by Cardinal Hume. He lies in his monastic habit, the pallium around his neck. Some distance away, St Benedict gazes into the night sky, seeing the glory of heavens and, I pray, the soul of our holy bishop moving swiftly towards his heavenly home. May he rest in peace. Amen.

Notes

1. D. Milroy, 'Hume the Abbot, 1963–1976' in C. Butler (ed.), *Basil Hume: By His Friends*, London, 1998, p. 12.
2. Fr O'Sullivan was a Westminster priest and philosophy tutor at the English College at the time of his sudden death from cancer in 1997.

This tribute to Cardinal Hume was included in the 1999 edition of 'The Venerabile', shortly after his death.

Cardinal William Allen (1532–1594), founder of the English Colleges at Douai and Rome

Afterword

Homily on the Four Hundredth Anniversary of the Death of Cardinal Allen (Sunday 16 October 1994)

Cardinal George Basil Hume, O.S.B.

Many of us here today are pilgrims. In a sense every visit to Rome is a pilgrimage. And being a guest in this house is entirely appropriate in that this was its original purpose from 1362. It was a place for pilgrims – until Cardinal Allen turned it into a seminary.

Let me speak about my journey here this time, happily not by air, but by car. So a visit to Lisieux was possible, with the consequent realization just how vital, and central, is a life of prayer. There seemed to be no other presence in Theresa's cell save that of God Himself. Then to Assisi, and a prayer before that Crucifix where Francis learned that he was to build up the Church – his apostolate to preach Christ, and Him crucified. Then to Rome.

How Allen travelled from the Low Countries I do not know. He first did so in 1567, with a canon lawyer and another companion. The former wanted to see Pius V about a project he had to convert the infidel. He never saw the Pope. It was Allen's second journey which was important. That was in December 1575. I think the Pope himself, Gregory XIII, had the idea first of founding a seminary here. Allen was to do it. And no doubt he had the same motive as that which prompted the foundation at Douay, namely 'to establish a college in which our countrymen, who were scattered about in different places might live and study together more profitably than apart ...', and furthermore, 'we feared that if the schism should last much longer ... no seed would be left hereafter for the restoration of religion ...'. That was surely a noble aim: to prepare young men for the universities and academic excellence, and this for the work of the Gospel. After all Allen was no mean scholar himself. He knew the importance of the academic and especially, of course, of a sane and orthodox theology.

But it was not scholars that he was to send back to England, and, let me add, Wales. No, not scholars, but martyrs. Come out of the refectory and their names are on the wall opposite; go up the stairs and they confront you once more. What a tradition! What examples of true devotion, strength of faith, steadfast courage! 'You had one idea, William Allen, but God had another. You thought of future scholars for a Catholic England, God wanted martyrs for a struggling community! Thank you, Your Eminence – though that title came later and for reasons more political than otherwise. Thank you for our seminaries.'

Allen had to come back in 1579 to sort out some rows; the Welsh and English did not see eye to eye. Our seminaries are peopled by human beings, doubtless with faults, with differences of opinion, none perfect. But where the eye's focus is on God problems do not divide, true community is formed. I know it to be thus here.

So my pilgrimage must go on for another two weeks or so. But the memories of the journey here linger on, not entirely, I must admit, without a sense of being reproached by Theresa, by Francis and, indeed, by Allen too. What about my prayer life? Do I preach Christ, crucified and risen, with passion for that central truth in order to build up the Church? What about that love of theology which should be part of my priestly life? What about my willingness to die for my faith? That is all for my examination of conscience.

What about you, today's seminarians, tomorrow's priests? St Mark records stern words of the Lord. Take them to heart. You are not here to seek yourselves and personal advancement. Like the Master who called you, you are not to be served but to serve others. That costs. It involves learning to pray; it means exploring the truth of Christ's death and resurrection upon which His Church is built; it is to be equipped intellectually to speak with conviction about God, about the Gospel; it means, above all, to have the heart of a martyr, strong, resolute, courageous. We need such priests today.

This is a good place. It has had many benefactors over the years, and today, surely, we remember with gratitude Philip Cardinal Howard, who shares this special year with William Allen. He died a century later.

Allen died on this very day, four hundred years ago, his pilgrimage through life completed. He rests here, precisely where we do not seem to know. No matter. He has an important place in the history of English Catholicism, and thus has to be remembered by us. Whatever his faults, Allen stands now, surely, 'before the throne of grace' (Heb. 4:16) in the very presence of Him who Himself had been through every trial (ibid. 15), Christ our example, our inspiration.

Cardinal Hume preached this homily at a Mass in the College to celebrate the 400th Anniversary of Cardinal Allen's death on 16 October 1994. It was originally published in the 1995 edition of 'The Venerabile'.

Select Bibliography

Anderson, Robin	*Rome Churches of Special Interest for English-Speaking People*, 1982
Champ, Judith F.	*The English Pilgrimage to Rome: A Dwelling for the Soul*, 2000
Duffy, Eamon	*Saints and Sinners: A History of the Popes*, 1997
Gasquet, Cardinal Francis Aidan	*A History of the Venerable English College, Rome*, 1920
Harvey, Margaret	*England, Rome, and the Papacy, 1417–1464: The Study of a Relationship*, 1993
	The English in Rome, 1362–1420: Portrait of an Expatriate Community, 1999
Kenny, Anthony	*A Path from Rome: An Autobiography*, 1985
Martin, Gregory	*Roma Sancta (1581) – Now first edited from the Manuscript by George Bruner Parks*, 1969

Munday, Anthony	*The English Roman life* (ed. Philip J. Ayres), 1980
Parks, G. B.	*The English Traveller to Italy*, 1954
Philpot, Tony	*A Short History of Palazzola*, 2001
Schofield, Nicholas and Whinder, Richard	*The Venerable English College, Rome: An Illustrated Guide*, 1999
Various	*The Forty-Four: Martyrs of the English College, Rome*, 2000
Various	The Beda Book: An Anthology, 1957
Williams, Michael	*The Venerable English College, Rome: A History, 1579–1979*, 1979
Wiseman, Cardinal Nicholas	*Recollections of the Last Four Popes and of Rome in their Times*, 1858